Stories of School Yoga

Stories of School Yoga

Narratives from the Field

Edited by

Andrea M. Hyde and Janet D. Johnson

Published by State University of New York Press, Albany

For information, contact State University of New York Press, Albany, NY
www.sunypress.edu

Library of Congress Cataloging-in-Publication Data

Names: Hyde, Andrea M., 1969– editor. | Johnson, Janet D., 1968– editor.
Title: Stories of school yoga : narratives from the field / edited by Andrea M. Hyde and Janet D. Johnson.
Description: Albany : State University of New York Press, [2019] | Includes bibliographical references and index.
Identifiers: LCCN 2018043672 | ISBN 9781438475691 (hardcover : alk. paper) | ISBN 9781438475707 (pbk. : alk. paper) | ISBN 9781438475714 (ebook)
Subjects: LCSH: Affective education. | Hatha yoga for children—Study and teaching. | Hatha yoga for teenagers—Study and teaching. | School children—Mental health.
Classification: LCC LB1072 .S86 2019 | DDC 370.15/34—dc23
LC record available at https://lccn.loc.gov/2018043672

10 9 8 7 6 5 4 3 2 1

Contents

Section II: National Programs

Section III: Working with Marginalized Populations

Acknowledgments

We wish to acknowledge the inspiration, guidance, and encouragement of those whose support was necessary for this project to come into existence. The motivation for this book came from the stories and experiences of yoga service providers and yoga teachers who bring yoga to schools every day.

We are indebted to Edi Pasalis and Iona Smith and the other organizers of the Yoga in Schools Symposium and Research Summit at the Kripalu Center for Yoga and Health, where we first met in 2015. We especially thank Sat Bir Khalsa, Catherine Cook-Cottone, and Tamar Mendelsohn for their continuing support for research on yoga in schools. We also acknowledge and thank Michelle Kelsey Mitchell and the other organizers of the National Kids Yoga Conference for providing a continuing community for us all.

The authors in this volume embraced the opportunity to share their stories with us and with the school yoga community. Their narratives are modest snippets from the important work they do, and we are grateful for their contributions to the field and to this volume. Their tireless and joyful advocacy for students and teachers through yoga is inspiring.

We received personal and professional support from our colleagues and institutions—Western Illinois University and Rhode Island College. Janet received a faculty research grant from RIC that allowed her to travel to work with Andrea in the Quad Cities. We are also grateful to QualRIC, a qualitative research group that provided extensive feedback on early drafts of the book proposal and beginning chapters.

We thank the reviewers who provided comprehensive and valuable feedback. Their words pushed us to do be more precise and aware of what was missing. We also thank SUNY editor Rebecca Colesworthy, who provided expert suggestions on revision and encouraged us to make this book into readable scholarship for multiple audiences.

We thank our families, particularly our husbands, who endured many evenings and weekends by themselves as we worked on this book together and alone. As readers, writers, and partners, their love and support was incredibly important. Thanks also to our fur-babies, Andy, Bailey, Mama Cass, Ozzy, and Silent Bob, who kept us company and, more importantly, reminded us to punctuate our sedentary work with snuggles, snacks, naps, and play.

And finally, we thank each other for friendship, collegiality, and hard-nosed scholarship. We pushed each other to extend our learning and examine our assumptions about yoga, research, theory, and social justice. We are better writers and researchers as a result of this partnership.

Introduction

"I Just Breathe": Stories of School Yoga

JANET D. JOHNSON AND ANDREA M. HYDE

> Yoga is a process of replacing old patterns with new and more appropriate patterns.
>
> —Sri T. Krishnamacharya

> When I'm really mad and like ready to explode, I just breathe. And every time I breathe out I just let all the anger out.
>
> —William, yoga student

High school youth trail into the basement classroom at 9 a.m., yawning as they tease each other or look at their phones. William sweeps one half of the classroom where chairs and tables have been pushed aside. The classroom teachers direct students to the free breakfast of packaged muffins and orange juice, and then to the computers lined up against the wall, where students log in to their individual plans. When Janine, the yoga teacher, arrives, bike helmet still on, the hum in the room gets louder. Students jostle each other as they move to unfurl their yoga mats into an uneven circle. "Miss, can I ring the chime?" Miguel asks. Janine hands him the chime, and class begins. When students are lying on their backs for the final resting pose 50 minutes later, the room is quiet and still until the morning announcements blast suddenly from the ceiling speakers, interrupting the peace. David, eyes still closed, gives an obscene salute to the disembodied voice.

This kind of scene (with or without the salute) occurs in hundreds of K-12 schools across the United States. The yoga-in-schools movement, along with the mindfulness in education movement, has gained momentum over the past several years as adult practitioners realize the benefits of yoga in their personal lives and want children and youth to have the same opportunity to experience them.

Because yoga attends to both mind and body, it supports student overall well-being, which has led to its use in schools across the country. Teachers use yoga-based mindfulness techniques to provide mental breaks and physical activity during instruction and as part of their classroom management approach to help students become more aware of their emotions and actions and, in turn, to self-regulate their behavior. ESL teachers show their students how yoga poses are universal across diverse languages. Counselors teach mindfulness practices to support self-calming and stress reduction for students with behavioral issues. Schools adopt yoga and mindfulness to enhance social emotional learning (SEL), health and physical education, and anti-bullying programs. Educators also use yoga-based mindfulness practices to support principles of inclusive classrooms as well as academic content standards for second language acquisition, development standards for Early Childhood, and universal ethics. Mindfulness and yoga also appear in higher education, as yogi-academics, including teacher educators like ourselves, use the practices in their classrooms to support learning and well-being.

Yoga and mindfulness in K-12 environments coincide with increased awareness of the stresses associated with teaching and learning in public schools, chiefly those that are underfunded and populated by students from low-income families who now make up the majority of public school children (Jiang, Ekono & Skinner, 2016). While these families may be loving and stable, with adults who value education, poverty carries a host of stress-inducing and time-consuming challenges in addition to financial deprivation. Poverty contributes to children's mental health problems with as many as one in five students showing some signs or symptoms of mental, emotional or behavioral disorders (Freeman & Kendziora, 2017, pp. 2–3). Meanwhile, an estimated one in four children suffers from some sort of abuse or neglect in their lifetimes (CDC, 2018).

The resulting trauma can have negative emotional, cognitive and physical health effects, often resulting in learning and behavioral issues. In order to address these issues, some schools have amplified their services, functioning as 24/7 community centers that provide mental and physical health services, adult education, and food supplementation. Some schools have resource professionals such as counselors, social workers, nurses, and behavioral specialists who, along with teachers, can support children and families. Many do not, however, placing additional demands on the primary school personnel. Although special education and language learning programs are required by law, many schools remain chronically underfunded and, arguably, the laws themselves come up short.

Even well-resourced public schools are controlled by state and federal mandates which dictate a curriculum insufficient for the well-being of many students. We are concerned that the current emphasis on narrowed curriculum and high stakes testing is also having a negative effect on public school students (Johnson & Richer, 2015). This general lack of autonomy limits teacher effectiveness and creativity, as teachers must often choose between meeting mandates and attending to their students' needs.

Our work as teacher educators and researchers focuses on compassion, empowerment, and social justice. As yoga practitioners and teachers, we experience and witness the power of yoga to transform, and believe that yoga should be available to everyone. We believe that students and teachers in public schools can benefit from the breathing, mindfulness, and movement techniques inherent in the yoga practices described in this book. We vigorously support public schools as one of the last spaces where people from different backgrounds gather to learn the principles and practices of democracy, which include critical thinking, group and individual human development, and creative academic and technological pursuits. We are encouraged by the latest reauthorization of the Elementary and Secondary Education Act (ESSA, 2015), which provides funds that can be used for social-emotional learning and health and wellness programs. While states have discretion on how the money is distributed, some districts have used it for school yoga programs.

As the school yoga movement grows, so does the need to understand how yoga works and its effects on individuals, groups, and school culture. However, few studies address the actual experiences of people involved in yoga programs because only a handful of qualitative studies on school yoga exist. Missing are the thick descriptions and stories that capture the conditions that lead to schools adopting yoga programs, how programs are planned, introduced, and implemented, what yoga teachers encounter in schools, and how they encourage students and school staff to embrace yoga practices. This book narrows that gap in the literature by focusing on the stories of those who bear witness not only to what happens during yoga, but what comes before and after, making meaning from yoga practices within specific school contexts.

The stories that yoga teachers tell about their experiences, observations, and interactions with children and adults have much to offer the growing field of yoga in schools, in addition to research on school climate and student engagement. The bulk of this book is written by contributors from a variety of K-12 contexts who share their discoveries and questions, joys and tensions in teaching yoga in schools. We asked them to write about what various stakeholders—from students to yoga teachers to school personnel to parents to policymakers—should know about school yoga. Their narratives illustrate the complexities of the school-yoga field, supplementing, questioning, and reframing current findings from more traditional, quantitative research. This provides crucial information for school personnel and yoga service providers planning to offer yoga in schools, while providing support for those already doing so.

The Organization of this Book

As an informational text, this book focuses exclusively on yoga programs operating in public schools. Yoga also happens in private schools, but we chose to bind the project's scope to the economic, political, and social public school environment, with its unique goals and constraints. While yoga is our central object of study, it also informs our methodology. Indeed, as a critical text, this book argues that a yogic approach to research, an approach like ours that focuses on feminist relational theory and narrative inquiry, is suitable for a wide range of qualitative research projects and evaluations of programs, yoga-based or not, especially programs serving historically marginalized populations. This approach, which we will describe at greater length in chapter 2, values participants' experiences and stories, particularly when participants serve as narrators of their stories, creating a reciprocal relationship between researcher and participant. It upends the traditional subject-object relationship in which the researcher holds all the power, and as we hope this demonstrates, can yield richer, more dynamic findings.

This book contains multiple voices through two distinct but related languages: one academic, one practical. We begin with the academic in chapter 1 by defining yoga and outlining the current state of school-based yoga research. We then contrast qualitative research with traditional scientific research, demonstrating how qualitative research methods are necessary for a comprehensive understanding of school yoga. In chapter 2, we outline our theoretical lens: yogic-ethical/feminist-relational, and explain how we are using narrative inquiry. We also acknowledge the particular challenges and limitations related to qualitative research in this context.

The heart of the book contains the voices of teachers, counselors, and yoga service providers who have developed programs and do the actual teaching of yoga in schools. They are experienced, knowledgeable educators, and some have advanced degrees in education or allied fields and/or national followings via their publications, trainings, and websites. By inviting our contributors to tell their stories, we mark their work as academic and practical knowledge production.

We organized these chapters based on how contributors situated themselves in their stories. Section I offers chapters by school-employed educators who have introduced yoga into their everyday school lives. Helene McGlauflin is a school counselor in Topsham, Maine, who details her move from focusing on diagnosing and treating student pathology to teaching children resilience and wellness through a yoga class she calls Calm and Alert. Inspired by the benefits of her personal yoga/mindfulness practice, Helene decided to explore whether an "inward focus, unity of mind, body and breath, and emphasis on wellness [could] adequately augment [her] mental health training" in teaching social-emotional development. Debra A. Krodman-Collins, a school psychologist from Broward County, Florida, describes how she developed S.T.O.P., a yoga-based curriculum for students with autism. She offers students stability and support in a world that can seem "mysterious, disjointed, and potentially dangerous." Lindsay Meeker, an ESL director in Illinois, shares how she changed her classroom management design to include yoga and mindfulness and shared these skills with colleagues. She developed breathing and movement exercises to work alongside her language arts skill-building to create a welcoming classroom environment for immigrant and refugee families.

Section II highlights three contributors who have developed national organizations. Lisa Flynn, based in Dover, New Hampshire, founded Yoga4Classrooms, a yoga and mindfulness program that promotes social, emotional, and physical wellness, learning readiness, and positive school climate. Lisa describes how she came to teach school yoga though painful personal struggles, founded a yoga service organization, and developed a train-the-trainer model of professional development to implement yoga and mindfulness practices schoolwide. Carla Tantillo Philibert, with co-author Peggy C. Collings, focuses on professional development programs for educators to grow students' social emotional learning (SEL) competencies with yoga through her company, Mindful Practices, which provides programs to students and teachers in mostly urban schools in Chicago. Dee Marie offers the origin story of Calming Kids, in Boulder, Colorado, which she founded to address bullying and to teach youth how to practice ahimsa, or nonviolence, through a classroom-based student yoga program. Dee details the initial resistance she encountered in the early 2000s to the present day, where Calming Kids's success enables her to offer teacher professional development workshops across the globe.

Section III focuses on yoga service providers who have extensive experience working with marginalized populations. Michelle Brook discusses the joys and challenges of working with youth in Title I (at least 40% of students receive free or reduced lunch) schools in Jersey City, New Jersey. Inspired by personal tragedy, she teaches children how to "build self-confidence and awareness to live happier lives by knowing how to regulate their own emotions." Joanne Spence, a yoga-based therapeutic social worker and founder of the nonprofit Yoga in Schools in Pittsburgh, Pennsylvania, began by creating yoga programs for health and physical education (HPE) classes on a district-wide scale. She describes her initial experiences with HPE teacher professional development and her move to teaching yoga as a holistic behavioral support in alternative schools. Peg Oliveira, a psychologist and child advocate in New Haven, Connecticut, teaches yoga as a way to raise consciousness for low-income, disaffected youth. Through her nonprofit organization, 108 Monkeys, Peg adapted her yoga teaching to urban high school students' strengths, needs, and expectations.

While we created these sections for easy navigation, readers will note plenty of overlap among the authors. All are white, middle class, cisgender women—a point we address at length in chapter 2. Moreover, all share an unyielding commitment to the profession and to students, even as they work in various contexts and with diverse populations across the country. There are also some key differences in how they approach their work, which we highlight in the codas and conclusion. We believe these variations showcase the necessary ambiguities of approaching and implementing this work in schools. The stories here demonstrate the importance of context when deciding on what form yoga programs will take, who should be the focus of instruction, and who should be the teachers.

Our final chapter is grounded in our feminist stance, in which we contextualize school yoga within the larger framework of social justice education and the ethical responsibilities of this work. We reflect on the entire project: our goals, the process of working with each other, and the use of narrative as a mode of inquiry to explore the current state of school yoga. In so doing, we explicate key themes from the chapters, and note what is absent or left unsaid. The most salient theme of this project is that *yoga in schools is about positive change.* We unpack this with a summary statement called "This is What We Know about Yoga in Schools."

References

CDC (2018). Child abuse and neglect prevention. Centers for Disease and Control. Retrieved from https://www.cdc.gov/violenceprevention/childabuseand neglect/index.html.

ESSA (2015). Every Student Succeeds Act of 2015, Pub. L. No. 114-95 § 114 Stat. 1177 (2015–2016).

Farrell, C., Fleegler, E., Monuteaux, M., Wilson, C., Christian, C., & Lee, L. (2017). Community Poverty and Child Abuse Fatalities in the United States. *Pediatrics, 139*(5): 1–11. Retrieved from http://pediatrics.aappublications.

Freeman, E. V., and Kendziora, K. T. (2017). *Mental health needs of children and youth: The benefits of having schools assess available programs and services.* Washington, DC: American Institutes for Research.

Jiang, Y., Ekono, M., & Skinner, C. (2016). Basic Facts about Low-Income Children: Children under 18 Years, 2014. New York: National Center for Children in Poverty, Mailman School of Public Health, Columbia University.

1

Qualitative Research and School Yoga

ANDREA M. HYDE AND JANET D. JOHNSON

In this chapter, we explain how we are using the term yoga, outline some of the current issues surrounding yoga in the schools, delineate key differences between qualitative and quantitative methods, and make the case for how this book contributes to the field of yoga research in schools.

What Do We Mean by Yoga?

As a philosophical system, yoga can be traced to practices arising in the Indus Valley more than 2,500 years ago. The first explicit references to yoga, though, did not arrive until the *Yoga-Sutra*, compiled by Patanjali around 200 to 250 CE (Hartranft, 2003). The *Yoga-Sutra* is a collection of observations on the nature of consciousness and human suffering. Many of the Sanskrit terms used today in yoga studios across the world come from this text. However, Patanjali describes a system of philosophical precepts and spiritual-contemplative practices, not the modern postural practices we think of today.

The *Hatha Yoga Pradipika* (Svatmarama & B. D. Akers, trans., 2004), written in the 15th century CE, is the first place where asana, or the physical practice of yoga, is discussed. The other attributes of hatha yoga are pranayama (breathwork), dhyana (meditation)—also practiced in yoga studios—and shuddhi kriya (cleansing techniques). The physical postures, developed by Indian yoga teacher Sri T. Krishnamacharya and popularized in the West by his students, B. K. S. Iyengar and Pattabhi Jois, are a modern creation related to early twentieth-century Indian physical culture during the British colonial period which influenced, and was influenced by, European gymnastics (Singleton, 2010).

While yoga evolved as a spiritual practice, it was not meant as a way to worship a deity, but rather a journey within the self. Interpreted as either restricting or balancing consciousness, the practices are meant for individuals to discover their true natures as consciousness turns inward, and for eventual release of attachments and liberation from suffering (Iyengar, 1966). In the current era, yoga teachers might ask students to focus on the breath, body, emotions, and/or thoughts as they go through the physical practice of asana. Yoga, as it is most often practiced in public schools in the United States, is a system of mind-body techniques that includes physical postures, conscious breathing, and deep relaxation, plus a kind awareness of the present, often called mindfulness (Butzer, Ebert, Telles & Khalsa, 2015).

Yoga in Schools: Benefits

Research with adults and youth in schools supports the experience of centuries of practitioners that yoga reduces stress and increases a sense of calm and focus, which contributes to emotional regulation and overall well-being (Beets & Mitchell, 2010; Frank, Bose, & Schrobenhauser-Clonan, 2014; Khalsa & Butzer, 2016). Public schools now frequently use yoga in physical education and health classes and as a way to support classroom management plans and/or social-emotional learning curriculums (Butzer, Ebert, Telles & Khalsa, 2015; Hyde & Spence, 2013). Teachers and counselors also use yoga as a behavioral intervention for children with attention problems and other emotional and academic difficulties (Delisio, 2009; Ehleringer, 2010). Yoga has been found to be particularly beneficial for teachers and students in high-poverty, adjudicated and clinical settings through lowering involuntary stress responses, building greater kinesthetic awareness, and increasing quality of relationships with family and peers (Kachtich & Anderson, 2009; Ramadoss & Bose, 2010).

Yoga in Schools: Controversy

Despite these documented benefits, yoga in schools is controversial for different reasons, depending on the audience. Some educators and parents are concerned that yoga's spiritual roots may be used to further a particular form of religion in secular public schools. Some critical educators, including us, worry that yoga is being used to keep students docile and obedient for the instrumentalist purposes of raising test scores, instead of for student well-being and social awareness. We explore these related controversies below.

Issues of Spirituality and Colonization

Because of its loose association with Hinduism, some parents have expressed fear that teaching and practicing hatha yoga in public schools violates the separation between church and state. The most well-known case is *Sedlock v. Baird*, which challenged the teaching of yoga in the Encinitas Unified School District in Encinitas, California. In 2013, the defense argued, and the court agreed, that yoga was a secular practice, which settled a suit brought by two parents against the Encinitas School District (Calamur, 2013). The opinion was upheld by the California Court of Appeals in 2015 (*Sedlock v. Baird*, 2015).

Although the Encinitas case was resolved in favor of the district, the case itself made yoga service providers and administrators more cautious about yoga in schools. In a qualitative study of the Encinitas School District, school personnel noted that they felt yoga had become political and created polarization in the community, thus making them more cautious about using yoga in schools (Cook-Cottone, Lemish, & Guyker, 2017). Even the word and actual practice of "yoga" is sometimes eliminated in favor of more innocuous terms such as stretching, calming, or focusing, because schools fear negative ramifications. For example, one yoga service provider we worked with recently removed all mention of yoga from its promotional materials and changed its logo, which originally was of a child engaged in Warrior II, a commonly recognized yoga pose.

Some scholars argue that yoga is being sanitized of its history in schools due to these fears. Removing the Indian cultural and philosophical foundations from the practice of yoga is a form of colonization that Westernizes an ancient Eastern practice, further denying the wisdom and utility of non-Western cultures as the U.S. curriculum too often does. Others are concerned that yoga is not presented as a spiritual practice. For yoga scholars and cultural critics, this cheapens yoga's history and potential for uniting mind, body, and spirit, thus making it just another form of physical education with some breathing exercises thrown in (Horton, 2016). For these reasons, groups such as the American Hindu Foundation and Decolonizing Yoga are pushing back on what they see as the whitewashing of yoga (Singh, 2013).

As yogis and scholars, we firmly support the teaching of yoga's history as both a philosophical/spiritual and a physical practice, and we are wary of presenting everything we do in schools as ahistorical, acultural, or apolitical. We also find that a segmented presentation of yoga shirks the ethical responsibility to "educate the whole child," which is necessary for a progressive, democratic society (Noddings, 2005). However, as educators who work in public schools, we recognize the concerns of school districts and yoga service providers, particularly in light of the *Sedlock* case. Several of our contributors describe their thinking about these dilemmas, demonstrating that there is no one-size-fits-all solution. Michelle Brook writes, "While I find this spiritual aspect of yoga meaningful, I don't feel that my public school students are somehow getting 'lesser' yoga than those I teach at a yoga studio, where I have freedom to share more spiritual yoga philosophy." Helene McGlauflin found it difficult to leave behind the language of yoga, but felt that it was more important that students learn the practices than to risk not being able to have yoga at all. We write more about this issue in the individual codas, as it is prevalent for most practitioners who engage in yoga in schools.

Dilemmas on the Purpose and Benefits of Yoga

Schools' instrumentalist focus on discernable, measurable results from students—usually measured by high-stakes tests—has had a clear impact on how yoga gets presented. Yoga and mindfulness practices are now often being exclusively referred to in terms of social and emotional learning (SEL) in order to justify their inclusion in the curriculum (Hyde, 2015). This has often meant the loss of the physical aspects of the practice. This is a strategic move to use legislated mandates to support programs that teachers and students want in their classrooms and to fund the practices and research. Even as we understand the need for yoga advocates and educators to demonstrate how yoga can address specific standards, we are concerned about the loss of the physical practice, especially since physical education and recess are often cut in favor of test preparation, most frequently in under-resourced districts (Beresin, 2013).

We also see red flags when yoga is promoted as a way to raise standardized test scores, similar to the way that it has been co-opted by some corporations as a way to increase worker productivity (Forbes, 2012). These instrumentalist aims pervert the self-care and personally transformative purposes of yoga. Yoga, depending on the intention behind it, could be just one more program based in capitalist, white, middle-class sensibilities to require youth from underserved communities to act in ways considered to be white. Thus, we need to be aware of the diverse ways that yoga practices are being used in schools.

Research on Yoga in Schools: Two Paradigms

Much of the current research on yoga in schools is traditional-scientific research, which relies heavily on quantitative data, such as pre- and post-surveys, or physiological measurements such as heart rate, to measure "causal relationships between variables, not processes," claiming "a value-free framework" (Denzin & Lincoln, 2005, p. 10) commonly known as quantitative research. Qualitative research, on the other hand, does not use variables or operational definitions, but rather relies on the researcher as an instrument of interpretation. The researcher studies phenomena in natural settings using a variety of empirical data, including case studies, personal experiences, observations, interviews, and other kinds of texts (Denzin & Lincoln, 2005). This is not to imply that qualitative research cannot be scientific in the sense of being systematic and rigorous. However, qualitative researchers do not seek to control study conditions or standardize and generalize results. Traditional-scientific researchers assume a position of objectivity, attempting to establish how and why yoga produces specific benefits from scientific measures, such as physiological responses. At the same time, they must acknowledge that even controlled measures (e.g., heart rate) are affected by context, attitudes, and the idiosyncrasies of human beings. As member of the Mindfulness in Education Network and professor of psychiatry, Allan Donsky, observes, "Science is not the only lens or paradigm by which we measure our lives. Science never was, and never will be needed to 'validate' the humanistic aspects of our existence such as kindness, compassion, mindfulness, forgiveness, alacrity, wisdom, heartfulness, joy, sorrow, elation and awe" (personal communication, August 17, 2015). We agree that traditional-scientific designs are limited by definition, and believe that qualitative research has much to add to existing studies.

Philosophy influences qualitative research because qualitative researchers are, at heart, philosophers (Denzin & Lincoln, 2005), examining beliefs about ontology (worldview, or theories of existence), epistemology (theories of knowledge) and methodology (2005, p. 27). When we engage in qualitative research, we are making a statement about our worldview, about what counts as knowledge, and about what knowledge is worth. Clandinin and Connelly write, "People are individuals and need to be understood as such, but they cannot be understood only as individuals. They are always in relation, always in a social context" (2000, p. 2). In keeping with our feminist-relational theoretical lens, elaborated further in the next chapter, the research in this book attends to the lived experiences of individuals, their relationships and the contexts that shape and are shaped by them. Instead of relying on quantitative measures, our research consists of narratives written by those with extensive experience in schools. Their stories serve as more than anecdotal data, in that they document the subtleties and nuances of the struggles and gifts of bringing yoga into schools. For example, Peg Oliveira describes how many of her students resisted doing yoga at first, and then eventually saw the practice as personally beneficial. She shares how one teenager turned her mat away from her friends and toward the wall in order to find balance. Peg realized that it takes time for adolescents to buy in to yoga, or anything introduced by adults, and that some students may never buy in at all. She concludes that this has to be okay.

Researchers at the 2016 Yoga in Schools Symposium, most of whom engage in traditional-scientific research, expressed concern that studies that relied strictly on quantitative data are not able to support specific claims about discrete effects. Further, it was noted that limited data may even be harming youth by further supporting biases (e.g., stereotype threat adversely affects performance) and advancing programs that don't really work, but seem to because of evidence of growth on self-report instruments or even on observable performance tests. Mark Greenberg, Endowed Chair of Prevention Research at Penn State University, suggested that first-person phenomenological studies and observations of interpersonal behavior are two additional and important ways for researchers to collect data, as these methods can help determine what and how to measure quantitatively (Greenberg, 2011).

Qualitative Research in Schools

Some of our colleagues who have worked extensively with randomized controlled trials are taking up qualitative methods, because, as Butzer, et al. (2017) conclude, "inconsistent quantitative findings suggest the need for a more nuanced investigation of the effects of school-based yoga" (p. 2). There have been very few strictly qualitative studies, but several teams have conducted what Lochmiller and Lester (2018) identify as "quantitative leading," mixed methods projects, where the researchers rely on a quantitative paradigm and privilege quantitative data, while using qualitative data to "deepen, enlighten, or explore particular ideas, concepts, or concerns" (pp. 216–217). This describes the work of Butzer, et al. (2017), Dariotis, et al. (2016), and Conboy, et al. (2013). Miller, et al. (2014) published an exploratory qualitative study as a formative assessment for a mindful yoga curriculum that was part of a larger, randomized controlled trial, which would be considered an "exploratory sequential design" (Lochmiller & Lester, 2018, p. 219) in which qualitative methods were used to inform the quantitative study. The only purely qualitative studies of public school yoga that we found in academic journals were by Finnan (2014) and Wang and Hagins (2016). These studies focused on youth experiences with yoga through surveys and interviews. Finnan found that students learned "important non-academic skills and attitudes related to focus, perseverance, and maintaining positive social relations"

(p. 27). She concluded that "the learning that takes place during yoga instruction is best treated as a social process involving a community of practice comprised of the yoga instructor, classroom teacher, and students, and that institutional support for non-academic learning experiences deepens student learning" (p. 26). With rich description of her observations and extended quotes from interviews, this ethnographic study shows how the non-academic lessons learned in yoga classes carried over into academic learning time in one school over time.

Wang and Hagin's (2016) study involved focus groups from the Sonima Foundation's Health and Wellness Program in four New York City public schools. Students reported that yoga helped them to regulate their emotions, be more mindful, reduce stress, increase self-esteem, and improve overall physical conditioning.

The research described above is valuable in showing program design and findings unique to qualitative studies. That said, these studies have been published in academic journals. Missing are the stories related on service providers' websites, in educator magazines, in graduate students' theses and dissertations, and those not recorded at all. For example, Andrea published a report on a two-year qualitative case study of an urban alternative school yoga program in *SAGE Research Methods Cases* (Hyde, 2017), a venue for work that models research and writing for graduate students. This was the only published report of the work that Joanne Spence (one of our contributors) did in this particular school, though there were several internal reports shared with the administration and one with an external funder.[1] We believe, and the stories in this book demonstrate, that there is significant information and unrecorded research that show tremendous variations in how yoga in schools is designed, implemented, and evaluated. For example, Deb Krodman-Collins's program focuses on working with students with autism individually and in groups, while Michelle Brook works with classes, and Carla Tantillo went from working directly with students to training teachers in how to use yoga in their classrooms.

Differences in Paradigms

For us, the differences between traditional-scientific research and qualitative research exist most markedly at the level of paradigm, or theory, including beliefs about the nature of reality and knowledge; the relationship of the researcher to the data; ethical action; and researcher biases, or subjectivity. The chart on pages 18–19 reveals some clear differences between qualitative and traditional-scientific research. Though some scholars still contrast qualitative and quantitative research at the level of methodology, we believe that methods are just one aspect of the differences between the research paradigms.

For practical purposes, there is every reason to be excited about the partnership between qualitative and traditional-scientific research in investigating the phenomena of teaching and practicing yoga in school settings. Qualitative researchers use literature reviews from quantitative studies, in addition to narrative descriptions and interpretive or critical analyses, to provide yoga program evaluations. Often, it is evidence produced through traditional-scientific studies on yoga and mindfulness that gets yoga educators access to the schools, as they are able to use the social capital of these studies to give their programs legitimacy. Traditional-scientific research also provides policy language to support yoga and mindfulness techniques as legitimate ways to address standards in various fields, such as health and physical education, social-emotional learning, classroom management and universal design for learning.

Why Use Qualitative Research in Yoga in Schools?

Unlike research labs, where predictability and control are paramount, schools are complex organizations filled with individual, dynamic actors. As public institutions, schools are impacted by outside forces, such as social and economic policies and community expectations, in addition to the school culture created and maintained by administrators, teachers, students, and parents. Qualitative researchers revel in the endless variations of human dynamics by studying individual and group beliefs, behaviors, stories, and interactions in their natural environments. Thus, qualitative researchers do not start with a hypothesis, but with a series of research questions which may evolve as we spend more time in a given context.

One of the core beliefs of qualitative research is that *all* research is biased, or subjective. Most of the people involved in researching the effects of yoga in school settings are yoga practitioners themselves. We have done first-person investigations on ourselves and found immediate benefits from doing yoga, and we want to share those benefits. We, along with others

Item	Qualitative	Traditional-Scientific (Positivist-Quantitative)
Nature of Reality	Multiple realities; subjective.	Single reality; objective.
Purpose	To understand & interpret social behavior & interactions.	To test hypotheses, look at cause & effect & make predictions.
Persons Studied	Individuals, smaller number of participants.	Larger groups or number of participants.
Selection of Participants	Purposeful, snowballed.	Random assignment or whole set (class).
Nature of Observation	Study behavior in a natural environment.	Study behavior under controlled conditions; isolate causal effects.
Focus of the Study	Study of the whole; everything is interesting; wide-angle lens; examines the breadth & depth of phenomena.	Specific variables studied; narrow-angle lens; tests a specific hypothesis.
Type of Data Collected	Words; images; scenes; objects and/or stories.	Numbers, responses assigned numerical value.
Data Sources	Interviews; observations; field notes; open-ended responses to questionnaires or focus group discussions; researcher's reflective journals and memos.	Pre/post tests; Closed answer self-report or observational inventories (structured & validated data-collection instruments).
Purpose of Data Analysis	Identify patterns, features, themes.	Identify statistical relationships; measure changes pre/post treatment.
Objectivity and Subjectivity	Subjectivity is expected.	Objectivity is critical.*

Role of Researcher Bias	Researchers and their biases may be known to participants in the study, and participant characteristics may be known to the researcher. Anonymity of participants is not always desirable.	Researchers and their biases are not known to participants in the study, and participant characteristics are deliberately hidden from the researcher (double blind studies).
Results	Particular or specialized findings that are dependable, consistent, confirmable.	Generalizable findings that can be applied to other populations.
View of Human Behavior	Dynamic, situational, social, & personal.	Regular & predictable.
Research Objectives	Explore; discover; construct; illuminate; empower.	Describe; explain; predict.
Final Report	Narrative report with rich contextual description & direct quotations from research participants.	Statistical report with correlations, comparisons of means & statistical significance of findings.

(Chart adapted from Creswell, 2013; Johnson & Christensen, 2008; Lichtman, 2006)

*However, even statisticians point out that numbers and statistics are subject to researcher bias: "Historical research has shown that what is studied, and what findings are produced, are influenced by the beliefs of the people doing the research and the political/social climate at the time the research is done" (Muijs, 2010).

(Berila, 2016; Douglass, 2011; Orr, 2002; Todd & Ergas, 2015), who are yogi-scholars and academics, have done work in comparing the language and philosophy of yoga with principles of feminist and critical theories. We will do more of that work in this book. In qualitative research, we can use that expertise. We can use everything we have, everything that conditions us as the primary instruments of inquiry, including our own yoga practices (Hyde, 2013; Janesick, 2004).

The expertise of the authors in this book comes from their study of yoga and lived experiences as yogis and teachers. Most certified yoga teachers have studied in one or more yoga traditions, so they know the history and the field-specific language of multiple forms of yoga. There is also a rich history of educational research involving teachers doing inquiry, making use of their insider knowledge and thus empowering them to create new knowledge (Falk & Blumenreich, 2005; Hubbard & Power, 2003). Andrea has found it quite easy to involve non-academic yoga teachers in qualitative research (Spence & Hyde, 2012; Hyde & Spence, 2013). She tells them to do what comes naturally to them: to be witnesses, observers, to be present with what is going on. Janet is a teacher researcher (Johnson, 2009) and teaches graduate courses in action research, where teachers systematize what they already do as professionals: observe, listen, and talk to students, and collect other forms of data. This "just do it" mentality—observe and collect data before bounding the context and forming research questions—is more common than not in teaching qualitative research methods (Lichtmann, 2009). For this reason, we find qualitative research to be an empowering kind of inquiry and one that is appropriate for yoga programs that have liberatory ends.

Yoga and Social Justice

Nowhere do we claim that yoga is a one-size-fits-all panacea that will fix public schools. We do not even assume they are broken, though we certainly acknowledge savage inequalities (Kozol, 1991) in how they are resourced. We advocate for pedagogically sound policies rooted in teacher autonomy to make room for high quality and varied instructional and curricular practices (Johnson & Richer, 2015); economic changes that reduce the number of people living in poverty (Anyon, 2014); and personal, public, and media practices to crack and dissolve systems of oppression. Even as we acknowledge oppressive systems, the authors in this book demonstrate the power of what yoga offers teachers, students, and school communities right now, in service of the above goals. We believe that yoga in schools can "be used to address oppressive ideologies and practices in the lives of students and thereby foster change not only on the intellectual level . . . but also on the levels of the body, emotion, and spirit" (Orr, 2002, p. 480).

In the next chapter, we describe our feminist theoretical approach and why we adopted it. We also provide an explanation of narrative inquiry and its appropriateness for this project.

Note

1. In general, students reported that yoga made them feel "good," "calm," "relaxed," or simply "better" (p. 5). Joanne and Andrea also found major barriers to providing more yoga to the students or setting aside time and space for self-practice (as they requested), similar to those expressed in the studies above, but with additional specific structural limitations of the school.

References

Anyon, J. (2014). *Radical possibilities: Public policy, urban education, and a new social movement* (2nd Ed.). New York: Routledge.

Beets, M. W., & Mitchell, E. (2010). Effects of yoga on stress, depression, and health-related quality of life in a nonclinical, bi-ethnic sample of adolescents: A pilot study. *Hispanic Healthcare International, 8,* 47.

Berila, B. (2016). *Integrating mindfulness into anti-oppression pedagogy: Social justice in higher education.* New York: Routledge.

Butzer, B., LoRusso, A. M., Windsor, R., Riley, F., Frame, K., Khalsa, S. B., & Conboy, L. (2017): A qualitative examination of yoga for middle school adolescents. *Advances in School Mental Health Promotion.* DOI: 10.1080/1754730X.2017.1325328.

Butzer, B., Ebert, M., Telles, S., & Khalsa, S. B. (2015). School-based yoga programs in the United States: A survey. *Advances in mind-body medicine, 29*(4), 18.

Calamur, K. (2013). Calif. Judge rules yoga in public schools not religious, NPR: The Two Way. Washington, DC.

Clandinin, D. J., & Connelly, F. M. (2000). *Narrative inquiry: Experience and story in qualitative research.* San Francisco: John Wiley & Sons.

Clandinin, D. J., & Connelly, F. M. (1998). Personal Experience Methods. In N. Denzin & Y. Lincoln (Eds.), *Collecting and Interpreting Qualitative Materials*. 150–178. Thousand Oaks, CA: Sage.

Conboy, L. A., Noggle, J. J., Frey, J. L., Kudesia, R. S., & Khalsa, S. B. S. (2013). Qualitative evaluation of a high school yoga program: Feasibility and perceived benefits. *Explore, 9*(3), 171–180.

Cook-Cottone, C., Lemish, E., & Guyker, W. (2017). Interpretive phenomenological analysis of a lawsuit contending that school-based yoga is religion: A study of school personnel. *International Journal of Yoga Therapy, 27*(1), 25–35.

Creswell, J. (2013). *Qualitative inquiry and research design: Choosing among five approaches, 3rd ed.* Thousand Oaks, CA: Sage Publications.

Dariotis, J. K., Mirabal-Beltran, R., Cluxton-Keller, F., Gould, L. F., Greenberg, M. T., & Mendelson, T. (2016). A qualitative exploration of implementation factors in a school-based mindfulness and yoga program: Lessons learned from students and teachers. *Psychology in the Schools, 54*(1), 53–69. DOI: 10.1002/pits.21979.

Denzin, N., & Lincoln, Y. (2005). Introduction: The discipline and practice of qualitative research. In N. Denzin & Y. Lincoln (Eds.), *The SAGE handbook of qualitative research* (pp. 1–32). Thousand Oaks, CA: SAGE.

Delisio, E. R. (2009, September 28). School adopts yoga for wellness, behavior management. EducationWorld.com. Retrieved from http://www.education world.com/a_admin/admin/admin575.shtml.

Douglass, L. (2011). Yoga as counternarrative: American higher education rethinks difference and interdependency. *Pedagogy, Pluralism and Practice, 15*, 1–35.

Douglass, L. (2010). Yoga in the public schools: Diversity, democracy and the use of critical thinking in educational debates. *Religion and Education, 37*(2), 162–174.

ESSA. (2015). Every Student Succeeds Act of 2015, Pub. L. No. 114-95 § 114 Stat. 1177 (2015–2016).

Falk, B., & Blumenreich, M. (2005). *The power of questions: A guide to teacher and student research*. Portsmouth, NH: Heinemann.

Finnan, C. (2014). Not a waste of time: Scheduling non-academic learning activities into the school day. *The Urban Review, 47*(1), 26–44. DOI: 10.1007/s11256-014-0286-5.

Forbes, D. (2012). Occupy mindfulness. Retrieved from http://beamsandstruts.com/articles/item/982-occupy-mindfulness.

Frank, J. L., Bose, B., & Schrobenhauser-Clonan, A. (2014). Effectiveness of a school-based yoga program on adolescent mental health, stress coping strategies, and attitudes toward violence: Findings from a high-risk sample. *Journal of Applied School Psychology, 30*(1), 29.

Greenberg, M. [GarrisonInstitute] (November 22, 2011). Nurturing mindfulness in families, schools and youth: Advancing the science and practice of awareness and caring. [Video file.] Retrieved from https://www.youtube.com/watch?v=R3KXkO7NeG0.

Hartranft, C. (2003). *The yoga-sutra of Patanjali: A new translation and commentary.* Boston: Shambhala.

Horton, C. (2016). Yoga is not dodgeball: Mind-body integration and progressive education. In B. Berila, M., Klein, & C. Jackson Roberts, C. (Eds.). *Yoga, the body and embodied social change* (109–124). Lanham, MD: Lexington Books.

Hubbard, R. S., & Powers, B. M. (2003). *The art of classroom inquiry: A handbook for teacher researchers.* Portsmouth, NH: Heinemann.

Hyde, A. (2015). Mind-Body Tools for Teachers: A Proposal for Incorporating Mindfulness Techniques into Teacher Education. *Teachers College Record*: September 28, 2015. Available at http://www.tcrecord.org ID Number: 18138.

Hyde, A. (2013). The yoga of critical discourse. *Journal of Transformative Education, 11*(2), 114–126.

Hyde, A., & Spence, J. (2013). Yoga in schools: Some guidelines for the delivery of district-wide yoga education. *Journal of Yoga Service, 1*(1), 53–59.

Hyde, A. M. (2012). The yoga in schools movement: Using standards for educating the whole child and making space for teacher self-care. In J. A. Gorlewski, B. Porfilio, & D. A. Gorlewski (Eds.), *Using Standards and High-Stakes Testing for Students: Exploiting Power with Critical Pedagogy* (109–126). New York: Peter Lang Publishing, Inc.

Iyengar, B. K. S. (1966). *Light on yoga.* New York: Schocken Books.

Janesick, V. (2004). *"Stretching" exercises for qualitative researchers.* Thousand Oaks, CA: Sage.

Johnson, B., & Christensen, L. (2008). *Educational research: Quantitative, qualitative, and mixed approaches.* Thousand Oaks, CA: Sage Publications.

Johnson, J. (2009). Teacher candidates' critical conversations: The online forum as an alternative pedagogical space. *Human Architecture: Journal of the Sociology of Self-Knowledge, 7*(1), 75–85.

Johnson, J., & Richer, B. (2015). "This is against American ideals": Rhode Island teachers respond to PARCC. *Teachers College Record.* Retrieved from http://www.tcrecord.org/Content.asp?ContentID=18146.

Kachtich, K., & Anderson, D. (2009). Peace on the inside: For kids in the juvenile justice system, yoga and meditation programs offer the rare and life-changing opportunity to find calm and comfort within. *Yoga Journal (October), 98*: 101; 120–122.

Khalsa, S. B S., & Butzer, B. (2016). Yoga in school settings: A research review. *Annals of the New York Academy of Sciences, 1373*(1), 45–55.

Khalsa, S. B. S., Hickey-Schultz, L., Cohen, D., Steiner, N., & Cope, S. (2012). Evaluation of the mental health benefits of yoga in a secondary school: A preliminary randomized controlled trial. *Journal of Behavioral Health Services & Research, 39*(1), 80–90.

Kozol, J. (1991). *Savage inequalities: Children in American schools*. New York: Harper Perennial.

Lichtman, M. (2009). *Qualitative research in education: A user's guide, 2nd ed.* Thousand Oaks, CA: Sage.

Lochmiller, C., & Lester, J. (2018). *An Introduction to Educational Research: Connecting Methods to Practice*. Thousand Oaks, CA: SAGE Publications, Inc.

Miller, S., Herman-Stahl, M., Fishbein, D., Lavery, B., Johnson, M., & Markovits, L. (2014). Use of formative research to develop a yoga curriculum for high-risk youth: Implementation considerations. *Advances in School Mental Health Promotion, 7*(3), 171–183. DOI: 10.1080/1754730X.2014.916496.

Muijs, D. (2010). *Doing quantitative research in education with SPSS*. Thousand Oaks, CA: SAGE.

Noddings, N. (2005). What does it mean to educate the whole child? *Educational Leadership, 63*(1), 8–13.

Orr, D. (2002). The uses of mindfulness in anti-oppressive pedagogies: *Philosophy and praxis. Canadian Journal of Education, 27*, 477–490.

Ramadoss, R., & Bose, B. K. (2010). Transformative life skills: Pilot studies of a yoga model for reducing perceived stress and improving self-control in vulnerable youth. *International Journal of Yoga Therapy, 20*(1), 75–80.

Sedlock v. Baird, 235 874 (Cal: Court of Appeal, 4th Appellate Dist., 1st Div. 2015).

Serwacki, M., & Cook-Cottone, C. (2012). Yoga in the schools: a systematic review of the literature. *International journal of yoga therapy, 22*(1), 101–110.

Singh, R. (July 9, 2013). Yes We Won and What We Lost: *Sedlock vs. Baird* Decision Allows Yoga in Public Schools. South Asian American Perspectives on Yoga in America (SAAPYA). Retrieved from https://saapya.wordpress.com/2013/07/09/yes-we-won-and-what-we-lost-sedlock-vs-baird-decision-allows-yoga-in-public-schools/.

Singleton, M. (2010). *Yoga body: The origins of modern posture practice*. New York: Oxford University Press.

Svatmarama, S. (2004). *The hatha yoga pradipika* (B. D. Akers, trans.). Woodstock, NY: YogaVida.com, LLC.

Todd, S., & Ergas, O. (2015). Introduction. *Journal of Philosophy of Education, 49*(2), 163–169.

2

The World Is Made Up of Stories

JANET D. JOHNSON AND ANDREA M. HYDE

As teacher educators, we teach prospective teachers in certification programs and classroom teachers in graduate programs. We are also qualitative
researchers and have similar epistemological and ontological perspectives,
although Andrea's work is based in the social and philosophical foundations of education, while Janet's work is in adolescent literacy, specifically English education. We belong to different professional organizations,
attend different conferences, and read different journals. That said, it was
easy to agree that feminist theories were the appropriate framework and
narrative inquiry was the most suitable methodology for this project.

A Feminist-Relational Approach

In recognition that there are multiple feminisms and that feminist theories
are always in process (hooks, 2000), we decided on a feminist relational
perspective (Campbell & Wasco, 2000; Ellis, 2007; Olesen, 2011). Feminist
relational theory offers two important features that ground our thinking:
first, it provides for an understanding of mutual recognition and value,
such that our contributors are partners in this book; and second, it "takes

as a given that women's gender-related experiences intersect with socio-economic status, race, age, ethnicity, sexual orientation, and other forms of difference that situate people in a socially stratified and hierarchical society" (Greenberg, 2007, p. 257). Even though our contributors may have the privileges that come with being white and middle class, they also encountered barriers based on their gender and the devaluation of their experiences in schools and as researchers.

In adopting a feminist-relational stance, we acknowledge that relationships are paramount to the work of yoga in schools and signal that we are operating under a strong ethic of care (Noddings, 1984). Yoga philosophy and feminist epistemology come from similar paradigms. Yoga is about conscious self-discovery: it is non-competitive and values compassion for others as well as the self. It is through accurately perceiving, and then accepting the self, that "discriminative awareness" (Freeman, 2010, p. 65) can arise. Yoga philosophy also recognizes the oppressive nature of social systems that seek to undermine individual lived-experiences for the sake of power, ownership, and competition. Instead of seeking power, yoga:

> allows us to experience the body as it is, to see the mind in its natural state, to see others as they are, to see the world around us just as it is. Good [yoga] philosophy encourages a full multiplicity of viewpoints, and it allows us to explore new perspectives. (Freeman, 2010, p. 211)

Similarly, feminist epistemologies are about understanding and valuing the knowledge, experience, and suffering of marginalized groups, particularly women. Taking a feminist perspective means that we, the editors, are self-reflexive, in that we examine our practices as teachers and researchers, such that we do not privilege traditional-scientific scholarship, or data, over individual interpretation of experience. The focus on relationships as complex rejects binary thinking (i.e., scholar or practitioner; theory or methodology; narrative or counter-narrative) in order to embrace a both/ and frame (Collins & Bilge, 2016).

Because feminist epistemology is an anti-oppressive way of describing and understanding human phenomena, it is appropriate for theorizing how yoga can serve to undermine the hierarchical paradigms that are currently in place in schools. Students, particularly those from underserved populations, are further marginalized by rigid curricula and constant, high-stakes testing (Hagopian, 2014). In this book, authors share stories of how yoga has provided students with agency to view themselves and others with compassion. As with many wisdom traditions, yoga is about the relationship to the self and the relationship to other. At its best, yoga offers students opportunities to see their strengths, a powerful antidote to how they are often positioned in schools.

Thus, we believe that yoga holds not just spiritual weight but political weight. Some of the authors in this volume write about their struggle to balance wanting to be true to yoga's spiritual roots with the knowledge that some parents and school personnel may see it as proselytizing. That said, their stories highlight their commitment to children's emotional and physical development, often in the face of resistance from parents, school personnel, and the students themselves. We see the authors' work as push-back against the current standards-based, efficiency model of schooling, and therefore a quiet political statement about valuing the well-being of children and youth over test scores.

Narrative Inquiry and Qualitative Research

We, too, are making a political statement by insisting that this book be considered valid research in the social science community, even as our data consists of stories and not measurements. To address the complexity of stories as data, we use two terms interchangeably: research and inquiry. We understand research to be the systematic collection of data following some logic of organization and analysis. As discussed in chapter 1, we contrast traditional scientific research, which takes an objective stance and uses quantitative methods, with qualitative research, which takes a subjective perspective and uses descriptive and interpretive methods. We recognize qualitative research as being paradigmatically and methodologically distinct from traditional scientific research.

We also use the term inquiry, which we understand as something broader that includes research, but is not necessarily as systematic, ends-oriented, or rule-bound. There is obvious overlap between qualitative research and inquiry as just described. The broad and varied constellation of qualitative approaches includes those that parallel traditional designs, such as grounded theory and case studies that use interview and observation as primary methods of data collection. At the other end of the spectrum, some researchers break with traditional research rules and use entirely internal, subjective methodologies, such as autoethnographies, personal histories, and arts-based approaches that challenge the format of research entirely (Paris & Winn, 2014).

Narrative inquiry falls somewhere in the middle and has been used as a method for collecting data and a way to represent findings for decades (Clandinin & Connelly, 1998). The purpose of writing and collecting narratives is to share and understand personal descriptions of an event, a person, a situation and/or a context. As educational researchers, we are interested in the details and complexities of situations and contexts of schooling which stories provide. Rachel Naomi Remen said, "The world is made up of stories; it's not made up of facts" (Tippett, 2016, p. 26). Narratives may be partial and subjective, but they also provide opportunities to see phenomena in new ways.

The yoga-in-schools movement is fairly new, but it is also robust. Quantitative studies have yielded some knowledge about how students perceive yoga, but the nature of what counts as data and who counts as researchers limits the scope of that kind of research. We knew that the knowledge and expertise existed, and narratives seemed like the perfect way to capture new understandings of the phenomena. Schaafsma and Vinz write, "Narratives often reveal what has remained unsaid, what has been unspeakable. It reveals the importance of context, reflexivity, difference, and multiple identities and perspectives. Narrative inquiry helps us to see more carefully and completely" (2011, p. 1). We believe that the stories in this volume offer important insights, including revealing tensions, as not all of the contributors have the same intentions, philosophies, or experiences of yoga in schools. As co-constructors of meaning through the theoretical codas, we point out some of those tensions as key aspects of understanding the complexity of yoga in schools. Thus, form and function work together reciprocally in narrative research (Schaafsma & Vinz, 2011).

Our Story

In further emphasizing the relational in our approach, this chapter is not just about methods, but is also about the process of putting together this book. We, Andrea and Janet, connected at the first School Yoga Research Summit at The Kripalu Center for Yoga & Health, a yoga center in western Massachusetts, as the only two qualitative researchers there. That year, 2014,

Andrea spoke on a panel, representing the voice of qualitative research as a divergence from an otherwise totalizing frame of traditional scientific research. She advocated for more qualitative work, pledging to help yoga teachers tell their stories and get their work recognized as field knowledge. Janet had been conducting a pilot study of a yoga program for youth of color in an underserved school. She attended the conference hoping to connect with other yoga researchers but was dismayed at the focus on quantitative methods, and then thrilled to connect with fellow qualitative researcher and new ally, Andrea. The following year, we were both invited to speak at the Research Summit as the only two qualitative researchers, although others were experimenting with mixed methods. Immediately after the conference, we hatched the plan for this book. Andrea has considerable experience researching yoga in schools, and Janet's background is in ethnographic inquiry in educational settings. As yogis and professors who work with teachers and youth, we believe in the physical, emotional, and cognitive benefits of yoga practices for everyone, no matter their age.

Collaborating on a coedited volume with multiple authors requires relationship-building and ongoing dialogue. Since we live a thousand miles apart, with Andrea in the Quad Cities and Janet in Rhode Island, most of our meetings were via FaceTime and over email and text. Janet visited Andrea during the earliest part of the project, and Andrea stayed with Janet for a few days the following spring. These visits, which included yoga classes, long walks, and dinners, shifted our relationship from collaborators to friends. This made it easy to be honest about our disagreements, accept each other's feedback, and engage in shared decision making. From long conversations on whether to use the term subjectivity or bias to shorter ones on comma placement, this collaboration required us to not only name our perspectives, but to provide evidence for them from our respective fields. These dialogues created the groundwork to share our different areas of expertise and come to consensus. The work of the book and the work of our growing relationship went hand in hand, which we see as crucial to a project grounded in feminist ontology and epistemology.

The Process of Gathering Narratives

In deliberately valuing relationships, we see the contributors in this book as partners, not subjects (Bhattacharya, 2017). As Michael Apple wrote about Patti Lather, a leading feminist scholar who inspired our writing purpose and style, "For her, all critical inquiry is fundamentally dialogic and involves a mutually educative experience" (Apple, 1991, p. x). We believe that our contributors' work is valuable and should be seen as research, and so we invited them to share their expertise through writing about their experiences with school yoga.

The contributors were invited to participate in this volume through two networks of yoga teachers and service providers, the Yoga in Schools Consortium and the Yoga Service Council. We also distributed flyers at the Yoga in Schools Symposium at the Kripalu Center for Yoga & Health in 2016. We knew that these groups would include those present at the 2015 Yoga in Schools Symposium, whose work-as-knowledge we had pledged to support. We also asked members of these groups to share the flyer with their professional networks.

In our Call for Proposals, we asked potential contributors to include a short bio; tell the story of how they came to yoga; describe their teaching population and community; share their hopes and goals; and offer what they learned from their work, especially what they wanted those involved or interested in yoga in schools to know. We accepted all eleven proposals that followed the stated guidelines, met our criteria (i.e., their experience was in public schools), and came in by the deadline. We were pleased that the proposals represented a cross-section of experience geographically in urban, suburban, and rural schools across the United States and came from contributors who served in different roles, i.e., insiders (counselors, social workers, teachers) and outsiders (yoga service providers and yoga teachers) in schools. That diversity is limited, though, in that all the contributors are white, middle-class, cisgendered women.

Coaching and Editing

After selecting the proposals, authors were asked to write 4,000–5,000 word chapters. At this point, we were unable to reach one of the contributors, and a second declined to write the chapter. We each read all of the chapters, but split them up for revision and editing. The contributors have more experience with yoga in schools than we do, whereas we have expertise in research in schools and writing for publication. We positioned ourselves as writing coaches, with both of us having extensive experience working with college students and Janet with teaching writing methods to pre-service and in-service English teachers. Andrea served as the primary editor and coda author for Lindsay, Carla, Lisa, Joanne, and Debra, while Janet acted in this role for Peg, Dee, Helene, and Michelle.

All of the authors had distinct voices and wrote narratively with use of dialogue and anecdotes to offer readers an entry into their respective contexts. During the first round of reading, we focused on eliciting more detail. The second and occasional third rounds were more about paragraph and sentence-level decisions. As writers with extensive experience receiving feedback as well as giving it, we knew that the best way to encourage revision was a mix of authentic appreciation and question asking.

In writing the codas, we took a critical perspective in analyzing the key insights of the chapters and contextualizing them within the existing world of yoga in schools. However, we took different approaches based on our inclinations as writers and our relationships with the authors. And though we established a template for writing the codas and collaborated on each other's work, we let our singular writing styles stand. Andrea made use of her personal knowledge of the women for whom she wrote, having spent more time studying the field of school yoga and working with its members. Janet had met some of the authors at school yoga conferences, but did not have relationships with them beyond email exchanges. Because of this, she read the authors' work as a collegial editor without a personal frame of reference. For some readers, this multivocal style may sound discordant but, in the end, we felt more strongly about showing this process than we did about creating symmetry. We say more about our approaches to editing in the book's conclusion.

Some Vexing Issues

As qualitative researchers, we do not make claims that this work can be replicated, as we are not trying to prove a hypothesis. We also do not pretend that the stories in this volume represent objective perspectives on yoga in schools. All of the contributors believe, as we do, that yoga has much to offer youth, even if we differ on the ways in which it is taught and toward what ends. One limitation of this project is that we wanted to appeal to a broad audience of yoga scholars, practitioners, service providers, and school personnel. We tried to walk the line between a more traditional qualitative study for scholars and a "how-to" book for practitioners. This required the both/and perspective noted above since we do not believe the line between scholars and practitioners is solid. This atypical design created extra work of finding the right publisher and in shaping a proposal that would communicate our intentions. However, qualitative research often confounds categorization and the products of such research take a very long time to write, placing this five-year project on par with its ambitions. In framing the stories as research, and thus the authors as researchers, we are honoring the long tradition of teacher research, or action research (Campano, 2007; Hubbard & Power, 2003). Consequently, this book could be seen as a hybrid of research, first-person narrative, and how-to advice.

Representation

While we reached out to members of the school yoga community in the United States through two national networks and our own connections, we are conscious of the voices not reflected in this volume: women of color, men, the differently abled, more members of the LGBTQ community, and teachers outside of the U.S., among others. The contributors in this volume reflect the larger population of yoga students and teachers across the United States—72% women, 70% college-educated, and 80% white (Murphy, 2014). Thus, we see the limitations of this book as mainly in scope: we only had so many pages, and there are lots of meaningful stories of school yoga that are not captured in this volume. Nevertheless, we must claim some culpability for not specifically seeking to incorporate stories from a multiplicity of social locations. In gathering narratives, we did not set diversity of class, race, ability, or anything beyond school and community context as a goal, a significant limitation to this work. Looking through the late proposals, we also recognize how our selection criteria may have served to exclude some potential contributors, however unintentionally on our part. Privileging applicants who "meet the deadline" is one seemingly innocuous way of limiting opportunities for participation to those with greater social privilege. Having crossed class boundaries when I (Andrea) entered the professoriate, I have always been acutely aware of how the cost of travel, fees, and lodging at conferences limits the attendance to mostly middle-class and white people. We recognize the role that these and other factors may have played here, too.

Because of these limitations, we see this book as part of a larger conversation about yoga in schools that involves many stakeholders who do not fit the common model of white women as yogis and teachers. The field includes organizations, such as the Holistic Life Foundation and Y.O.G.A. for Youth, which are led by people of color with significant influence on the school yoga movement. As the movement continues to become more diverse, we hope to join with organizations, studio owners, and yoga service providers to ensure that those voices gain a significant place in this growing community, and, hopefully, to conduct further research with those who have been marginalized from mainstream yoga. We also return to issues of race and gender in the conclusion, where we discuss how the contributors in this book, while relatively privileged in some respects, are marginalized in others.

We are also missing student perspectives, except as interpreted within the contributors' narratives. While this was by design, in that the aim of this book was to hear practitioner perspectives, student voices would have added some texture and counterpoint. We have good reason to believe that more educational researchers are recognizing the importance of listening to students' experiences (Butzer, et al., 2017) and we are actively engaged in this work ourselves. We address these limitations in further detail in the conclusion.

We Do What We Can: A Focus on the Personal and Local

One of the defining features of qualitative research is that its methods allow for themes to emerge from the data under consideration, which are the frames or ingredients of understanding. In narrative research, themes emerge organically from the stories of participants and are always mediated through the interpretation of the researchers and, ultimately, the readers. The stories in this volume are layered. There are the personal stories of the contributors and how they came to yoga, the stories of bringing yoga to schools, and the stories of the children and youth with whom they work. They are all narratives of attempts to heal wounds brought about by an often unkind and impatient world. Remen said, "We are all healers of the world . . . It's not about healing the world by making a huge difference. It's about healing the world that touches you, that's around you" (Tippett, 2016, p. 25). The authors in this book sought to address the suffering they saw in students and refused to allow constraining systems to keep them from working toward positive social change. Their stories offer guideposts to others who are meeting structural resistance or logistical barriers in bringing yoga and other contemplative practices to schools.

Individually and collectively, these chapters demonstrate that there is no one right way to implement a successful yoga program in schools. So much depends on context, support, and, sometimes, a little bit of magic. Many of the contributors in this book mention that serendipity—being in the right place at the right time with the right people—catalyzed their work. Even as they often have to fit yoga into the nooks and crannies of the school day, their stories demonstrate yoga's value to children, and often to their parents, teachers, and school leaders. This grassroots sensibility can, perhaps, lead to systemic change in making school a more accepting and compassionate place for all students.

References

Apple, M. (1991). Introduction. In P. Lather, *Getting smart: Feminist research and pedagogy with/in the postmodern* (pp. vii–xii). New York: Routledge.

Bhattacharya, K. (2017, August). Why I HATE broccoli and other contemplations. Keynote given at the Summer Session for the Contemplative Mind in Society conference.

Butzer, B., LoRusso, A. M., Windsor, R., Riley, F., Frame, K., Khalsa, S. B. S., & Conboy, L. (2017). A qualitative examination of yoga for middle school adolescents. *Advances in School Mental Health Promotion*. DOI: 10.1080/1754730X.2017.1325328.

Campano, G. (2007). *Immigrant students and literacy: Reading, writing, and remembering*. New York: Teachers College Press.

Campbell, R., & Wasco, S. (2000). Feminist approaches to social science: Epistemological and methodological tenets. *American Journal of Community Psychology, 28*(6), 773–791.

Ellis, C. (2007). Telling secrets, revealing lives: Relational ethics in research with intimate others. *Qualitative Inquiry, 13*(1), 3–29.

Freeman, R. (2010). *The mirror of yoga: Awakening the intelligence of body and mind*. Boston: Shambhala.

Greenberg, S. (2007). Re-examining empathy: A relational-feminist point of view. *Social Work, 7*, 251–259.

Hagopian, J. (2014). *More than a score: The new uprising against high stakes testing*. Chicago: Haymarket Books.

hooks, bell. (2000). *Feminist theory: From margin to center*. Cambridge, MA: South End Press.

Hubbard, R., & Power, B. (2003). *The art of classroom inquiry: A handbook for teacher researchers*. Portsmouth, NH: Heinemann.

Lipman, P. (2006). "This IS America" 2005: The political economy of educational reform against the public interest. In G. Ladson-Billings & W. Tate, *Education in the Public Interest* (pp. 98–108). New York: Teachers College Press.

Noddings, N. (1984). *Caring: A feminine approach to ethics and moral education*. University of Oakland: California Press.

Olesen, V. (2011). Feminist qualitative research in the millennium's first decade. In N. Denzin & Y. Lincoln (Eds.), *The Sage Handbook of Qualitative Research* (129–146). Thousand Oaks, CA: SAGE.

Paris, D., & Winn, M. (2014). *Humanizing research: Decolonizing qualitative inquiry with youth and communities*. Los Angeles: Sage.

Schaafsma, D., & Vinz, R. (2011). *Narrative inquiry: Approaches to language and literacy in research*. New York: Teachers College Press.

Tippet, K. (2016). *Becoming wise: An inquiry into the mystery and art of living*. New York: Penguin.

Section I

Yogis on School Staff

3

One School,
Calm and Alert

HELENE MCGLAUFLIN

This is the story of one practitioner in one school who has utilized yoga and mindfulness to serve the adults and children in that community. It has been my hope to use the practices as a method for teaching children the self-regulation skills they need to learn and flourish, and to nourish and reduce stress in the adults who teach and serve children in the demanding environment of a public school. Mine is not a story of saving or transforming the world, but of encouraging one small world to breathe more deeply, move more skillfully, and think more positively.

I serve this community as a school counselor by contract, a yoga and mindfulness teacher by ethical choice, and a writer by vocation. Let me explain: 25 years ago I received my Master's degree in counselor education and have always practiced in a school; nine years ago I became a certified yoga teacher, drawn to bring the practices to the people I serve; and here I am as a writer, given this special opportunity to tell you the story of what has happened at the Woodside Elementary School since I first rang a chime.

The Beginning

At the beginning of the century, I had been in public education in various roles for 20 years, a school and a clinical counselor for 10, and a yoga/mindfulness practitioner throughout most of my adult life. As an elementary school counselor, I had been trained to consult with administrators, parents, and teachers about the mental health needs of adults and children; counsel children in order to develop social, behavioral, and coping skills for success at school; and coordinate meetings, enriching events, and interventions to help students grow. As a clinical counselor, I had been trained to understand, address, and treat pathology. As a yoga/mindfulness practitioner, I was developing a commitment to self-care through taking personal responsibility for mindful movement, thoughts, and actions. I was also developing a deeper yearning to alleviate suffering for the people I serve. What I came to see through the sometimes disparate lenses of these fields greatly troubled me. First, rapidly increasing demands on students and struggles to develop needed skills; second, a focus on pathology, rather than resiliency and wellness; and third, a lack of, and struggle for, wellness in the adults who serve children.

The Demands of the Public School Environment

I am a dedicated public educator who has always felt proud of the essentials a school community offers children: a place to belong, a midday meal, clothing if needed, caring adults, learning and growth. Though these remain, the practices of this century have brought demands that are at times too developmentally taxing to maintain a healthy balance for children. These demands include assessments that continue relentlessly throughout the year; an outward focus on academic and behavioral performance and levels of achievement; a decrease in time spent in unstructured, imaginative play; and higher expectations for children to focus, attend, and produce. Not surprisingly, what has emerged is a noticeable struggle in children to meet these demands, manifesting as weak emotional and physical self-regulation, underdeveloped social skills, inadequate stamina for demands, and fatigue. Sadly, I found myself part of a system that created a serious imbalance with consequential difficulties for our most precious charges, who I wanted to help with all my heart. A personal/professional metanoia began: I would have to create a helping path for myself that brought balance and health to children and those who serve them, or I would have to leave the system.

The Struggle for Wellness

As my commitment to my own wellness developed through practice, my desire to help others "be well" also grew. I began to see with some poignancy and alarm the yearning many educators had to be well and seek wellness for their students, and the barriers and threats to this desire. There was/is the intense pace of the school day which places demands that make meeting basic needs difficult, such as relaxed, adequate time for eating, drinking water, bathroom use, and restful refreshment, such as being still without a demand. There was/is the daily exposure to the contained spaces with more germs than should be named. There is the lack of time for writing sub plans and the lack of substitute teachers, discouraging rest at home when exhausted or unwell. There is the heartbreaking reality of feeling devalued: low pay, lack of support from families, inadvertent folly in the system that sabotages effort through constant change. As I lay in my own Savasana, I dreamed of offering every student, teacher, and parent such rest.

I turned to my yoga/mindfulness practices as possible antidotes, stress relievers, skill developers, perspective changers, and beacons of hope for my school community. I set an inquiry: could the practices, with their inward focus, unity of mind, body and breath, and emphasis on wellness adequately augment my mental health training, which increasingly appeared insufficient to adequately meet the growing needs of the children and teachers I was dedicated to serving in a public school?

At this time, I was also witnessing within myself a desire to turn toward the strengths, wellness, and resiliency of children, which led to a new perspective on the mental health and educational field's sometimes appropriate, other times over-emphasis on pathology. More children with diagnoses, more children on psychotropic medications as young as 5, more parents seeking help and feeling helpless about their skills to raise their children, more teachers discouraged about disruptive behaviors, more time spent at meetings focused on what was wrong, rather than what was right about a child. I found myself wanting to bring the hope of positivity to teachers, parents, and the children.

The Weaving of Worlds

Much has happened in the last fifteen years toward supporting the integration of yoga in the schools, such as respected research, research-based programs, and positive press. But at the time I began, there was not a Best Practices for Yoga in Schools (Childress & Cohen-Harper, 2015) offering standardization, and some controversy, both locally and nationally. I was aware I was considering weaving two different worlds together—the world of a public school with its curriculums, time demands, rules, regulations and stress, with the world of yoga with its movement, breath, respect, positivity, and relaxation. I had some exposure to those already reaching out from the yoga tradition, sailing into a school as a ship to a new land, with unexpected cultural surprises. I had my knowledge base and years of experience as a public educator creating inquiry questions and my concern about how to weave the yoga practices into a possibly welcoming, probably questioning culture.

Consequently, I knew I was in a unique position as I began. I had my faith in the practices, my ethical considerations as a professional, and my desperation as a helper. My bedrocks were the trust I had already developed within the school community and my commitment to longevity at this one school. These perspectives and foundations held me as I began and continue to nourish myself, and it is with gratitude that I list them here: my own daily practices and ensuing training; my supportive, like-minded principal; the trusting teachers and parents in the community; the growing body of research in yoga and mindfulness for children; the receptivity of the children and adults who practice with me; and the town of Topsham that has employed me throughout the process. All of these allowed me to relax into the journey slowly, carefully, and with awareness.

For the teachers, administrators and parents, I was seeking a comfortable approach to create safe yoga/mindfulness experiences to reduce stress, convince them of their efficacy, and avoid controversy. For the children I was seeking a safe, explicit approach to developing mind and body states that would encourage self-regulation, reduce stress, and increase the enjoyment of learning.

The Practices

In the early years before I sought formal yoga teacher training (2008 and 2010), I did three things consciously. First, I slowly integrated practices in my office with students on my counseling caseload. I started teaching children calm breathing, simple poses, and the power of positive thoughts. Second, I communicated transparently with parents, teachers, and administration about the practices using non-controversial language, including descriptions such as "utilizing mind, body and breath to teach skills for success," creating handouts and calling parents to describe the practices. Third, I attempted to keep current with the research in the fields of yoga for children, mindfulness for children, social/emotional learning, self-regulation, and executive function. These fields spanned the worlds I was bringing together, and would ensure protection from harm, for me as a teacher, for the program I was developing, and for my students.

The children in my office received the practices more enthusiastically than I expected: they enjoyed the movement, took learning the breathwork seriously, and were excited about learning how their minds work. Most impressively, these practices were effective. Upset children would visibly calm when taking a deep breath, impulsive children could successfully sit still as they listened to the sound of a chime, and even the youngest children could tell me how they "changed their muddy thoughts to clear" with a smile. It was all very promising, and I yearned to broaden my scope of influence to include more students and staff.

I found myself struggling as a teacher, however. What should I to do when a child says the breath made her dizzy? Did I teach a child's pose correctly? What do I really know about brain science? Do I persevere with children who say the practices are hard or uncomfortable? These questions led me to pursue the 200 hour Yoga Teacher Training at Kripalu in 2008, and Yoga Ed training in 2010. This knowledge base gave me the confidence and skills I needed to step off of my office-only mat and into the classroom and school culture.

To honor the worlds of school counseling and yoga I was weaving, I developed a class for students that would use yoga and mindfulness as a method to teach the self-regulation of what has been termed learning-related social skills (McClelland et al., 2000) rather than teaching yoga as the primary goal. I used the framework of a yoga class to develop 30-minute classes which I called Calm and Alert, words chosen carefully to describe optimal states for learning that reflected the goal of the class and would appeal to a school community. I envisioned the class in classrooms where students and teachers spent their days together, so children would practice on a mat in the place they would later practice off their mats and teachers would feel the energetic benefits of the class for themselves and their students in their own space. Simultaneously, I began offering a free weekly Kripalu yoga class for teachers to encourage wellness and comfort with the practices.

I chose the safest and least controversial aspects from the yoga field due to the newness of the field and documented controversy in public schools that can halt a program based on parent concerns that the practices are religious. These non-controversial aspects include: a deep respect for teaching, learning, and creating a partnership between teacher and child; the instruction and practice of mindful movement; the relaxed, calming atmosphere of a class; the imagery from nature; and the principles of healthy exertion and rest. Throughout the practice, I wanted the children to be attuned to themselves, relaxed even when challenged, with their bodies, minds, and breath free to serve them most optimally. These benefits from the yoga field have been more enjoyable and universal for the children than I ever imagined. Because my program uses yoga elements and skills rather than claims to teach yoga, this approach has been comfortable and transferable for the entire school community while maintaining the integrity of the practices.

It was also my responsibility as a school counselor to design and implement programs based on research and best practices in the field of social/emotional learning. The respected Collaborative for Academic, Social and Emotional Learning (CASEL) recommends effective teaching practices for skill mastery be "sequenced, active, focused and explicit" (Payton et al. 2008, p. 6). Calm and Alert classes are:

- sequenced through the unit areas of respect, calm, alert, learning times, transition times, social times;

- active through continual mindful movement; focused through highly engaging instruction; and

- explicit through clearly defined skill targets in movement and breath, as recommended in yoga teacher trainings.

That first year, I piloted the Calm and Alert class in all first grades for 28 weeks. I chose this grade level because of the enthusiasm and support of the teaching team, who anticipated a challenging incoming group. The second year I broadened the scope to include the kindergartens and second grades, with the hope of better mastery of self-regulation for all students by age 7. Although I knew all classes would benefit from the original 28 weeks of the pilot, guarding my own self-care and balancing my other duties led me to prioritize. I currently offer 30 weekly classes in kindergarten to firmly establish the practices in the first year of school and 6 to 10 classes in the fall for grades 1 and 2.

After experimenting for a number of years in grades 3 through 5 with various ways to continue the practices, I currently teach 4 of what I call "applied" Calm and Alert classes without mats in September of grade 3, which includes a review of the skills, and explicit teaching about when to use the skills throughout the school day. In grades 3, 4, and 5 I have grouped 2 to 6 lessons on positivity, attitude and mindset, kindness, self-management, and other enrichment experiences (such as mentoring and aspirations) under the umbrella "Call to Care." I borrowed this term from the Mind and Life Institute's initiative (2016), but use it specifically to teach caring about learning and those in a learning community. In every lesson I use breathwork, mindful movement, and activities that foster self-awareness, and I see that this brings depth that only the yoga and mindfulness field can offer. This consistent, yearly dedication by one teacher has helped the practices become established in the school culture: every classroom now has a Zen chime and many have student "chime helpers" who lead the class in what we call the "chime practice" (chime, 3 breaths, chime) when there is a need; "take a deep breath" is common language; and if there ever were an emergency, any teacher could say "stand like a mountain" and most children would become steady immediately.

Although the practices were very new and sometimes foreign in the early years, it was anecdotally evident that there was a thirst, in both students and teachers, for the practices. Rather than rushing out to make photocopies, the teachers stayed while I taught, watched the class, and took notes. Teachers asked how to "do calm and alert" themselves, and thanked me for "forcing them" to stop and take a breath.

Children regularly asked me in the hallways when I was coming again, told me they taught their little brother the "book breath" or could be heard singing the "calm and alert song" at recess. Most outstanding was the love the children showed for rest, always asking "will we have that rest again?" and wiggling with excitement as we laid on our mats at the close of every class.

Within a few years, the school saw an improvement in students' abilities to self-regulate by using calming breaths, doing child's pose in a "take a break" area, or by asking for the chime. Most exciting was the generalization of skills taught in class to many settings: an upset child in the nurse's office taking deep breaths, children in line "standing like a mountain" or a child at recess saying to a peer in a conflict, "You need to calm down right now." In addition, the school saw a reduction in office referrals and aggressive incidents, which we suspected was due, in part, to the instruction from the class with our youngest students.

There have been many surprises. My fear of controversy was quelled by an outpouring of support from parents and teachers. The power of the simple, deep breath to change an individual child or teacher's mood and the energy of a whole class was evident to everyone. The amount of instruction needed to teach children to prepare for practice: safely moving tables, taking mats from a bin outside their room, peaceful conflict resolution for sharing space as mats are rolled out. How truly uncomfortable some practices are for the most behaviorally challenged students, the ones teachers would say "need it most." How explicit instruction in unifying mind, body, and breath works so well for young children. How my modeling the deep respect a yoga teacher brings to all aspects of teaching and learning nourished the teachers and taught the children the true meaning of the word respect, weakened with overuse in the school setting.

Measuring the Effectiveness of the Practices

Ethically, it has been critical for me to support the development of the classes and practice with some kind of data. The field is in its infancy, and I am implementing a program whose effectiveness is still in question. I also feel vulnerable in my lack of training as a researcher, and isolation in a state with few established school yoga programs.

I began by conducting an action research study, using survey and anecdotal data from grade 1 teachers and parents in 2009, the pilot year of the Calm and Alert Class. The teachers and parents surveyed were asked whether there was observable evidence of skill mastery in various settings of school and home. I was most interested in discerning whether the Calm and Alert skills were being used by students throughout the school day in classrooms, the cafeteria, playground and specials or at home and extracurricular activities. Results were promising. The group as a whole showed improvement in self-regulation at various times of the school day, and individual students exhibited skill mastery and generalization in a number of instruction areas (McGlauflin, 2010).

Since that time, there have been open inquiries and ethical considerations for me in gathering data. Since 2010, there has been a yearly, exponential increase in the amount of time each school day teachers spend assessing students, collecting data, synthesizing data, and recording data in multiple ways, in multiple places, and about multiple academic areas. It is a highly stressful situation for teachers and students, an unhealthy practice. I have sincerely felt I could not, in good conscience, ask teachers to collect more data in the current climate without addressing these concerns.

Another challenge in developing measures is the large number of variables and influences on student behavior and skill use in a public school setting. With appropriate humility, I am just one of multiple adults in the school teaching skills, cueing children to use skills, handling problems, influencing behavior. There are also innumerable variables that can influence behavior, such as: a child having enough sleep and food to practice self-regulation; substitute teachers that inadvertently change routines and the amount of limit setting; adverse childhood experiences. Such is the challenge for social scientists!

I have consequently relied on the following comfortable data tools. First, observation of individual students, whole classes, and the entire student body by myself, teachers, parents, and administrators, reported anecdotally. Second, data about "learning behaviors" collected three times per year through a screening tool used at the school called "Universal Screening for Learning Behaviors (USLB)" which is often used to grade students on work habits on the report card. It measures student performance in the areas of Safety, Respect and Responsibility. Third, the reduced number of office referrals for discipline and behavior slips that document inappropriate behavior. Fourth, in 2017 I developed a simple, 12-item assessment tool teachers could fill out while I was teaching their students. This has reduced the stress for teachers of "finding" time to complete the assessments, and promises to be more accurate through immediate assessment.

I have also been offered research partners. In 2016 the school district conducted the Gallup Poll of Hope, Wellbeing and Engagement of fifth through twelfth graders, and the Woodside School scored higher than all other schools in the district in 8 of 13 areas, and high in every area. More specifically, in 2015 a social work intern conducted a case study of the Calm and Alert Program by interviewing 12 teachers on the efficacy, challenges, and overall perception of the class. The results were generally positive, with teachers reporting enthusiasm for the class's effectiveness in "helping them teach" by explicit instruction in self-regulation. There were many supportive comments about me as a practitioner, the comfortable way the practices have been brought to the school, and the "culture of calm" it has created (Perkins, 2015). While these results were gratifying as a teacher, objectively, it raised my awareness of the school's possible over-reliance on one practitioner implementing a program designed and maintained by just the originator. It puts the long-term sustainability of the program at risk. The publication of my book, *Calm and Alert: Using Mind, Body and Breath to Teach Self-Regulation and Social Skills to Children* (2018), or further training of teachers or a successor could help remedy this risk.

Finally, the recent publication of *Best Practices for Yoga in the Schools* (2015) has been most affirming and relieving for me. It has addressed the inquiries, concerns, and vulnerabilities I have faced, and created a protective standard. The editors and contributors are the master weavers that I have so needed for my tapestry, and I thank them.

The Fruits of Practice

Like most fruits after years of practice, those most evident at this one school are small, simple and now quite ordinary. But when I or others notice them, I feel a spark of joy for the quiet extraordinariness of these beautiful gifts to the school community.

- Lanky, olive-skinned Jessie asked me after class, "Where did you get your chime?" I told her and asked her why she wanted to know? She replied: "I am asking for a chime for Christmas because my family is crazy and I want to use it with them."

- Red-haired, freckle-faced Luke, age 5, who had many challenges controlling his body, hated the class with a passion at the beginning. He could not stay on his mat, complained fiercely every class, and refused to follow any directions for weeks and weeks. By the 28th week, he could stay on his mat more than half the time, could follow half the directions and, best of all, would ask when we were having class again because "now I like it."

- Hank has a round face with dimples and wire-rimmed glasses, and a special condition that creates the difficulty of poor eyesight, too much weight, and emotionality about small things. He would cry often and say, "I can't do it." I would often smile and say, "Oh but you can, I know how hard it is. Let your breath help you." After many weeks, there was one class where he still cried, but loudly took breaths and said, "I am doing it."

- Talkative, always worried Marly, age 6, saw me and said, "My dad is in the hospital because he had too many muddy thoughts, and needed help," which I later learned referred to a psychiatric hospitalization. The concepts of "clear" and "muddy" thoughts helped her understand what was happening for her dad in a non-judgmental way.

- Lunch chime: Debbie the cafeteria teacher oversees sometimes 120 noisy, wiggly children in the lunchroom multiple periods a day, and uses the practice of the chime, three deep breaths, chime, before lining the children up. The setting is anything but ideal: as she guides the practice the microphone creates static, the chime sound is brash, her reminders to breathe might have an edge and at best, only half the students are attentively practicing. But the few who are practicing are earnest and serious, their bodies visibly moving up and down with the inhale and exhale. Their small calmness offers to bring the noise, the chaos and sometimes pandemonium down just a notch so that someone can finish a sandwich in peace. Debbie says, "When I am frustrated, I get out the chime, and feel like it is something I can do."

- Recently, blue-eyed, dark-haired 7-year-old Bryce stood at a whole school assembly and led the student body in what we call the chime practice. Although usually challenged in exhibiting self-control, on this day and with perfect composure he said into the microphone, "Sit up straight" then struck the chime. All 340 students were still as the sound lingered. He then said "take a deep breath in," waited, then "take a second deep breath in" then "take a third breath in" and the community visibly calmed. Next he struck the chime again, and all listened. This was one small, visible fruit of more than a decade of carefully bringing yoga/mindfulness practices to a public school: even the most challenged child can practice, and lead a practice; the students practiced, no longer needing instruction, only cueing; the entire community treated the practice with respect and the benefits were visible; and it is an established, routine practice known by the whole school community.

Janet's Coda

In this chapter, Helene McGlauflin addresses the limitations of her clinical training and positivist measures in determining, respectively, the need for what yoga practices offer and how to measure their effectiveness. She beautifully illuminates the very issues this book seeks to address: describing and analyzing the complexity of school-based yoga, and using narrative as a way to demonstrate its value to children and adults.

By focusing on, as she puts it, "one practitioner in one school," Helene shows us the universal and unique aspects of context. She became alarmed at the increasing demands placed on students and adults in her school, and how the resulting issues were being pathologized, or blamed on the students, instead of bringing attention to the system itself. Her observations of these effects are echoed in critical educational research that examines how current neoliberal policies blame the students and teachers for failures that are rooted in inequitable systems (Gorski, 2016; Horton, 2016; Nolan, 2011). Helene clearly states her ambivalence about working within this system, while also wanting to support children who did not have the power to leave it: "A personal/professional metanoia began: I would have to create a helping path for myself that brought balance and health to children and those who serve them, or leave the system."

In addition to naming and wrestling with this particular tension, Helene also explicitly describes why she chose to focus on elements of yoga, such as breathwork, mindfulness, movement, and rest, without naming the class as a yoga class. In so doing, she sought to avoid controversy in providing practices that she believed would be beneficial to students.

This brings up one of the paradoxes that many yoga service providers experience: how to balance the discomfort some parents and school personnel may feel about yoga's spiritual origins with the potential benefits. Horton (2016) argues that positioning yoga as another exercise with added stretching and breathing mitigates its true potential, and I (Janet) see her point. At the same time, I also applaud Helene's strategic literacy practices (Hines & Johnson, 2007) in working within the system she has been given. She clearly knew what would work in her community, and, as a result, she received full support from parents and school personnel instead of needing to defend what she was doing.

Helene is fully aware that the sustainability of the program was dependent upon demonstrating positive results through research. She notes that there are multiple variables that could account for improved student behaviors in classrooms and social spaces and fewer office referrals. Through adding observations and developing a specific measurement tool for teachers, she has expanded the effectiveness of more generic tools.

For me, perhaps the most salient feature of Helene's chapter is her recognition that, all too often, programs like these are overly dependent upon the originator. If the originator leaves, the program is in danger of being cut. She offers solutions, including teaching the practices to teachers and writing her own book, but the larger question remains: is yoga in schools here to stay, or is it yet another program in the constant churn of change that has inundated public education for decades? Helene's chapter asks multiple provocative questions of yoga-in-school advocates.

References

Childress, T., & Cohen-Harper, J. (Eds.). (2015). *Best practices for yoga in schools*. Atlanta, GA: Yoga Service Council/Omega Publications.

Gorski, P. C. (2016). Poverty and the ideological imperative: A call to unhook from deficit and grit ideology and to strive for structural ideology in education. *Journal of Education for Teaching, 42*(4), 378–386. DOI: 10.1080/02607476.2016.1215546.

Hines, M. B., & Johnson, J. (2007). Teachers and students as agents of change: Toward a taxonomy of the literacies of social justice. In D. Rowe, R. Jimenez, D. Compton, D. Dickinson, Y. Kim, K. Leander, & V. Risko (Eds.). *2007 Yearbook of the National Reading Conference*. Oak Creek, WI: National Reading Conference.

Horton, C. (2016). Yoga is not dodgeball: Mind-body integration and progressive education. In B. Berila, M. Klein, & C. Jackson Roberts (Eds.). *Yoga, the body and embodied social change* (109–124). Lanham, MD: Lexington Books.

Nolan, K. (2011). Oppositional behavior in urban schooling: Toward a theory of resistance for new times. *International Journal of Qualitative Studies in Education, 24*(5), 559–572. DOI: 10.1080/09518398.2011.600263.

McClelland, M., Morrison, F. J., & Holmes, D. (2000). Children at risk for early academic problems: The role of learning related social skills. *Early Childhood Research Quarterly, 15*(3), 307–329.

McGlauflin, H. (2010). The calm and alert class: Using mind, body and breath to teach the self-regulation of learning related social skills. Educational Resource Information Center, ED511066. Retrieved from http://www.eric.ed.gov.

McGlauflin, H. (2018). *Calm & alert: Yoga and mindfulness practices to teach self-regulation and social skills to children.* Eau Claire, WI: PESI Publishing & Media.

Mind and Life Institute. (2014). Call to Care Year in Review. Retrieved from http://www.mindandlife.org/care.

Payton, J., Weissberg, R. P., Durlack, J. A., Dymnicki, A. B., Tayler, R. D, & Schellinger, K. B. (2008). The Positive Impact of Social and Emotional Learning For Kindergarten to Eighth Grade Students. Collaborative for Academic and Social Emotional Learning. Retrieved from www.casel.org.

Perkins, S. (2015). Case Study of Calm and Alert: Teacher Reflections on a Mind-Body School-Based Intervention at Woodside Elementary in Topsham, Maine. Unpublished graduate capstone project report: Biddeford, ME: University of New England.

4

S.T.O.P. and Relax

A Yoga Curriculum for Students with Autism

DEBRA A. KRODMAN-COLLINS

I imagine you want to make a change for the better. Change can be hard to handle. My own life turned, along with the century, in 1999.

I am a school psychologist passionate about children whose disabilities impair their capacity to manage emotions and behavior. Where some seek to avoid or control a child who is viewed as stubborn, unreasonable, and unmanageable, I endeavor to comprehend and assist a child who is misunderstood.

Imagine that the everyday material and social experiences you take for granted are, instead, mysterious, disjointed, potentially dangerous. The blades of a ceiling fan create a staccato rhythm of light that might be fascinating—or terribly irritating. The rumble of a dishwasher, the itch of a clothing tag are unbearable, even painful. Perhaps you have not mastered language at all, or can only echo the sentences you hear. If you do communicate in words, you take them literally, expecting people to say precisely what they mean. Social cues elude you; you miss them or misinterpret them.

A sound, a touch, a word can trigger tremendous anxiety. The world is a minefield! To feel safe, you depend on the predictable and familiar. You like information and activities that are unambiguous. One plus one is always two. A square is never a triangle. If you are able to role-play at all, the dialogue and actions must match the video that inspired your play. You insist on unchanging routines.

Your comfort zone is so narrow. A definite breach, or the last straw in a series of tiny events, triggers survival defenses: FIGHT or FLIGHT. Your parents and teachers don't understand why "out of nowhere" you are shouting, crying, running away, hiding, flailing, throwing objects, hitting, kicking. Their attempts to calm or control you do not work. They become wary, alert for your next meltdown. Now everyone is walking in a minefield.

Once upon a time, students with such problems, for example, students with autism, were confined to special education programs kept separate from "the mainstream." In 1997, however, the Individuals with Disabilities Education Act (IDEA) mandated that free, appropriate public education be provided in the least restrictive environment that meets a disabled child's needs. This had a profound effect on school systems, including Broward County Public Schools (BCPS) in Florida.

Discovering Yoga as an Antidote to Stress

Broward County, Florida, is famous for fun—relaxing Fort Lauderdale: sunny beaches, cruise ships, college students enjoying spring break. I work here. It's hard work, requiring adaptability. The district is impressively diverse. BCPS is the sixth largest district in the United States, with about 270,000 students in over 300 schools. About 90% of students are black or white, in roughly equal proportions; the remainder are multiracial, Asian, or Native American. Approximately one-third claim Hispanic heritage. Forms are routinely printed in Spanish, Creole, and Portuguese, as well as English. Interpreters are available for Mandarin, Urdu, Malayalam, and more. Most students qualify for free or reduced lunch (about 60%). About 10% lack English proficiency, and about 10% are in special education. The district does not survey religious affiliation, but the county is dotted with an expansive variety of churches, synagogues, and mosques.

BCPS embraced the mandate for inclusion. My elementary school welcomed students with autism disorders. Autism is a "spectrum" disorder, meaning there is a wide range of symptoms, skills, and severity. Along the spectrum, these students exhibit impaired ability to communicate and interact socially. They show strong, often rigid preferences for specific routines and interests. They may exhibit odd patterns of behavior, including withdrawn, "self-stimulating" behaviors such as repetitive rocking or other movements.

The school set up four self-contained classes for these students and placed aides in general education classes.

According to their needs, the students spent their days in a self-contained class, a general education class, or some proportion of each. These students also took the high-stakes state achievement tests from which previously they had been exempt.

A hallmark of autism is severely limited adaptability. These students were pioneers in an unfamiliar school with unfamiliar teachers, staff, peers, and expectations. Meltdowns were frequent. The fight/flight behaviors could be dramatic and unsafe: hiding in a cupboard, running away, throwing furniture, hitting children, kicking adults. Sometimes a child recovered composure only upon becoming physically exhausted.

Meanwhile, my psychologist colleagues elected me Team Leader, their resource person for clinical advice. Without warning, the department supervisor left. The vacancy remained unfilled for months. Suddenly I was the go-to person for anyone needing anything to do with Psychological Services. At home, I was abruptly and unexpectedly going through a divorce. Every child and adult around me depended on me.

My tears, anxiety, and anger threatened my own meltdown. Fortunately, unlike my students with autism, I could ask for help.

It was surreal. I, a psychologist, was sitting in the patient's chair in a therapist's office. The counselor listened attentively. "Go to yoga," she said.

This was a novel concept in 1999. I lived near Fort Lauderdale, not the Red Fort of Delhi. "A studio, Joy of Yoga, just opened," my counselor explained. "Go."

Unfurling a borrowed mat in a beginner's Hatha class, I surrendered to the teacher's directions for 90 minutes. I "practiced" things I took for granted. Breathe. Bend. Straighten. Sit. Turn. Breathe. I came back once a week, twice a week. My life swirled like a hurricane—but on the mat, I rested within the calm, the eye.

Amazingly, the eye found a place within me. I started to see differently. There was something we'd overlooked, something central to our students with autism. Jayson's movements were lethargic, but stiff. Sam seemed to curl into himself. Amy darted about, unable to settle. Tension pulled at Manny's muscles even when he was supposedly at rest. Dave often was on the verge of hyperventilating.

I felt a new empathy. My own anxiety and stress were not only mental, they were physical. Yoga practice was teaching me that I'd been unaware just how much tension I carried in my breath and body. Suddenly it was obvious that we had disregarded the children's physical tension, even though it was clearly visible. They were physically primed for a meltdown well before any specific event triggered one.

None of the interventions in place to minimize meltdowns addressed this elephant in the room. We reduced environmental distractions. We structured the classrooms, provided visual schedules and communication tools, and made simple, illustrated stories to explain situations new to the children. We systematically rewarded desired behaviors, but this worked only when the students were calm. When agitated, they did not make contingency-based choices. They reacted, strongly and defensively. They could not "calm down" on command, or even to earn a reward.

I knew of programs that directly involved students in managing their own stress. There were checklists for children to identify personal triggers, and scales for them to rate the intensity of their feelings. To use these, a child had to be able to differentiate anger from anxiety, relaxation from stress, emotion from behavior. These methods required vocabulary, insight, and planning skills beyond the scope of our students.

I sat with Sally Miller, a special education teacher serving as the school's "autism coach." Sally had begun to take Hatha yoga classes, too. I shared that my limited experience already was affecting me powerfully. In the midst of unusual family, work, legal, and financial stresses, yoga provided an intensely fulfilling oasis of relief and equanimity. Sally said her experience was as palpable as mine.

Observing the children's posture, breathing, and movement through our new "yoga eyes," we agreed that even at their best, our students were never truly relaxed. No matter what we did to minimize triggers, they remained chronically on edge.

Hatha yoga would be a great fit for our students. The children would not have to talk or plan. Poses such as Table and Cat corresponded with concrete, familiar objects and animals, concepts accessible to students with limited vocabulary and abstract thinking.

We felt confident that yoga would improve our students' well-being in a profound way, empowering them. Their teachers and parents also would become more relaxed, by the same dynamic that presently cycled stress from the children to the adults and back again. Everyone would be more engaged, more productive, and, we believed, happier. Promoting the resilience and optimism of people we knew and cared deeply about, this prospect excited us and inspired Daniela Morales, a teacher in a self-contained classroom, to join our project.

Gaining administrative support and funding for yoga at school was another matter. "Yoga" was an esoteric term associated with religion. Public schools most definitely preclude religious instruction. Efforts to explain that Hatha practice was not religion would waste time and energy.

Mindful that school districts demand "evidenced-based" interventions, we looked for research to cite. We found nothing on teaching yoga in schools, or to children with autism. However, June Groden (1989, 1994) was teaching relaxation to children with autism, using exercises that tensed and relaxed muscles. Herbert Benson (1975) described the autonomic nervous system, showing that cognition and engagement are disrupted by fight/flight reactions but supported by the "relaxation response." We called our yoga project "relaxation training."

District administrators focus on district goals. Effective instruction, demonstrated by test scores, is an overwhelming priority. We explained that our students would be taking high-stakes state achievement tests for the first time. The pressure on the teachers and students would trigger plenty of meltdowns. We couldn't say whether test scores would increase, since there were no prior test scores for comparison. But we could enable our students to cooperatively take the tests.

Our project was approved!

The S.T.O.P. Program

We needed a yoga teacher. By a chance, seemingly arranged by the universe, Joy of Yoga held a party for students and staff. There I met Louise Goldberg. Louise is not only a yoga teacher, she is also a yoga therapist. In the past she had provided "creative relaxation" at BCPS's secondary school for students with severe emotional disturbances. Clearly she was interested in special needs, and she had district clearance for outside contractors working with students.

Louise enthusiastically joined our team. She contributed therapeutic voice, touch, purpose, and sequence of yoga postures. Sally and Daniela were expert in TEACCH[1] instructional methods such as visual cues, clarity of tasks and transitions, and effective prompting and reinforcement. Sally, Daniela, and I could write social stories (Gray, 1993): a short story written and illustrated to guide a child's understanding of the behaviors expected in a specific social situation (such as visiting the library or going on a field trip). I adapted cognitive-behavioral methods for managing anxiety, promoting relaxation, and generalizing new skills. Teachers completed rating scales before and after the eight weeks, we took students' pulse rates taken before and after the yoga sessions (after acclimating them to the setting and procedure), we videotaped sessions, and I compiled anecdotal reports recorded by ourselves, teachers, and parents.

Our space was a small office Sally and I shared. We cleared it as much as possible, in order to use the floor and, therefore, enable a full range of yoga positions: standing, seated, on hands and knees, prone, and supine. We could accommodate three students and three adults. Louise instructed, with two other team members assisting and collecting data. We scheduled two groups of students, three times per week. Sessions were 30 minutes, matching the time allotted for "specials" such as physical education. We met regularly, after school hours, to review progress and make adjustments.

The students chosen for the project had frequent stress episodes. Jayson, Ricky, and Manny, from a self-contained class, had limited verbal skills. Jayson was easily overwhelmed; often he withdrew. Ricky watched the clock, preparing himself for the next transition and highly agitated if it did not occur on time. Manny lacked patience and acted out aggressively. Amy, Dave, and Sam, with stronger verbal skills, were included in the general education setting. Amy was restless, flighty, easily distracted. Dave's little frame pulsed with anxiety; his breathing was shallow and rapid. Sam often was oppositional. Their parents gave written consent on permission slips we created for relaxation training.

I devised a rating scale, delineating observable physical, emotional, and behavioral signs of stress such as muscle clenching, crying, and loss of temper. Teachers' ratings for each child showed the severity of each indicator. We hoped that the post-program ratings would show reduced frequency and intensity of these indicators.

Louise, Sally, and Daniela collaborated to structure the setting and lessons, integrating principles of yoga therapy and TEACCH. Our students found predictable routines calming, but could become so fixated on a sequence that any deviation was intolerable. It was vital to balance familiarity and flexibility. Basic rules and transitions for initiating and ending sessions were outlined, such as removal and placement of shoes, staying on the mat, being quiet, and following the teacher's directions. Lessons started with "Huh" breaths, drawing attention to breathing and initiating a release of tension (shoulders draw upward on the inhale and drop with an open-mouthed exhale, "Huh"). Lessons ended with Cloud (Savasana). Within each lesson, the specific poses and sequences varied.

The first sessions were held eight weeks before the state tests. Soft, tonal music and soft lighting created an atmosphere conducive to relaxation. Louise provided simple spoken instructions and modeling. Two of us assisted, providing additional modeling and spoken or physical prompts. The students understood where to put their shoes and responded to reminders to stay on their mats. But they did not do the yoga poses.

Evidently they needed more effective cues. So, while Louise instructed and modeled a pose, we showed a photograph of her demonstrating it. Excited, the students focused on irrelevant details: "That's Miss Louise! That's her red hair!" They responded to the photographs as enjoyable images of someone they knew, not as models to imitate.

We tried stock photographs of children in the postures. We tried colorful illustrations that Sally drew. The children struggled to make sense of these images of persons unfamiliar to them: "Who is that? Is that a boy or a girl? I have a blue shirt, too! I see eyes. His mouth looks funny."

Sally rendered the poses in gray tones, with blank faces: not silhouettes, but quite muted, containing only those details required to show the position of head, torso, and limbs in relation to the mat. From the first one, the students immediately organized their bodies into the desired position. It was magical. These pictures successfully communicated forms to be imitated, not people to be understood. To this day, people unfamiliar with autism are disappointed that our pictures are not vibrant. Autism educators say, "Spot on."

With our students actively practicing, we began counting pulse rates as a direct, physical marker of success in improving relaxation. Having no mechanical devices, we took pulse rates by hand. To reduce risk of bias, one of us took starting rates and another took ending rates, varying our roles in each session and recording our counts independently.

Positive changes emerged more rapidly than we anticipated. Within about eight sessions, students showed visible increases in physical stability and flexibility. Jayson had wobbled in Table pose; now he balanced steadily in Table, with one arm raised. Amy's eyes and limbs were not darting about so much. Her Candle pose was increasingly vertical. Manny showed greater range of motion. Dave's breathing was deeper and more regular. We obtained parents' permission to videotape sessions, realizing that the images would help us demonstrate progress.

Students now responded to spoken instructions to "tense" or "relax" a muscle. We encouraged them to relax a tense muscle dramatically, rather than gradually. This maximized the difference they felt, making the contrast between "tense" and "relax" especially meaningful. When the children were supine, we placed little stuffed animals on their tummies. A child learned mindful diaphragmatic breathing by accomplishing a gentle rise and fall of the animal. They loved the "spaghetti test." While a student relaxed in Cloud pose, we gently lifted an arm by the wrist. The greater the relaxation, the more the arm drooped like overcooked spaghetti.

Most glorious was seeing a child resting peacefully in Cloud, experiencing deep relaxation for the first time.

Our students were creating calm and relaxation on the mat, in a quiet room with relaxing sensory cues. Could they learn to utilize their new skill amidst the challenges of the school day? We needed a prompt, meaningful to the students, useful to all staff, and to parents.

When these children cried, fled, or acted out, adults typically commanded them to stop what they were doing. Telling children who are acting from visceral stress to "stop" is not very effective. These children are reacting, not thinking about their behavior. Hearing "Stop!" does not shift their nervous systems from fight/flight to calm.

We transformed "Stop" into a useful cue: a signal to perform a well-rehearsed self-calming routine. S.T.O.P. became our acronym for a four-step routine incorporating muscle relaxation, diaphragmatic breathing, and posture. Using the letters and picture cues, S.T.O.P. prompted students to initiate a Soft face and shoulders, Take five slow, deep breaths, Open the chest, and check their Posture. Sally drew an illustration for each step. We practiced S.T.O.P. in every remaining yoga session. We made posters, laminated portable cue cards, and created a social story about doing S.T.O.P. when feeling stressed in class. Teachers and parents attended an evening session to see what the students were accomplishing and learn how to use this cue.

Our final videotaping was in preparation for that evening workshop. With the camera recording, Manny asked for a tissue to wipe his nose. There were no tissues in the room. Daniela had a paper napkin and offered that instead. For Manny, this was a catastrophic divergence from expectation. His reaction was fight, not flight. Shouting, "NO! NOT A NAPKIN! A TISSUE!" he advanced toward Daniela, about to lash out. Stating, "Manny, do S.T.O.P.," Daniela and the other adults present recited and modeled the four steps. Manny joined in and calmed himself. There could be no better demonstration of success.

The students had completed about 24 sessions when the state tests were administered. There were no behavioral outbursts during testing.

We reviewed the data we had collected. Results of the stress checklists and pulse counts were positive (Goldberg, 2004). Fewer signs of stress were reported for each student, with an average reduction of 7.75 points. The difference between the average pulse rate before and after the relaxation sessions was statistically significant ($p < 0.01$). Reviewing the videos, Louise pointed out evidence of deeper breathing and improvements in balance and stillness. Anecdotal reports confirmed that students were using the self-calming skills "off the mat."

Students responded to the S.T.O.P. cue. For example, I found Dave in the hallway, crying and fretting. He had fled the classroom. Dave did S.T.O.P. with me. Calmed, he was able to verbalize his fear of a spelling test. He accepted reassurance and returned to the classroom understanding he would have help.

Students used S.T.O.P. by themselves! Ricky, who precisely timed the routine events of his day, had meltdowns whenever the morning school bus was late. One late-bus morning, however, all was quiet. Ricky's mother looked for him, thinking he must be ill. She found him reclining peacefully on the sofa. "I am relaxing," he told her.

Amy's dentist finally was able to take impressions of her teeth. Amy spontaneously used the four-step sequence to calm herself for the procedure. Her mother was thrilled and grateful.

We could not keep this to ourselves. Children with autism, everywhere, deserve the "superpower" of relaxation as a skill to help them navigate the world. They deserve it NOW. We bypassed the hurdles of advocating for yoga for these children, and for acceptance of yoga in schools. We created something teachers anywhere could use, without expensive or extensive training. Something accessible, affordable, immediately useful.

Teachers can follow a curriculum. So can support staff such as school psychologists and occupational therapists. We refined our methods and materials to make a structured curriculum, S.T.O.P. and Relax.

It has instructions, lesson plans, visual cue cards, posters, stories, music, and progress-monitoring tools. Lessons are adaptable: they can be short or long, basic or advanced, tailored for preschoolers or young adults. Teachers in the United States, Canada, Europe, Asia, and Australia use it. Feedback is positive. Most recently, a premier preschool for children with autism obtained grant money to make S.T.O.P. and Relax part of the daily curriculum.

Making the Most of S.T.O.P.

As a school psychologist, I've since been assigned to other elementary schools. I take S.T.O.P. and Relax with me. These days, yoga is ubiquitous. Principals, teachers, parents, even students ask if the program is yoga and are pleased it is. They view yoga as a form of exercise, limited to postures and breathing. No one has raised inquiries or concerns about other aspects of yoga. Other aspects are not part of S.T.O.P. and Relax, anyway.

The principal and support staff help choose classrooms or groups to participate. Whether I pull a small group (by grade) or go into a classroom, the purpose is to reach children with significant difficulty regulating impulses and emotions. Some have an autism disorder. Others are diagnosed with attention deficit disorder or mood disorder. Some have no medical diagnosis or special education designation, but do have frequent outbursts or meltdowns. With parent permission, weekly 30-minute sessions become one of the rotating "specials" in their schedule.

The classrooms usually lack open floor space, so practice is limited to seated and standing postures. The first such venture was a fifth-grade class that included general education students needing instructional accommodations and special education students with learning disability, language impairment, emotional disturbance, attention deficit, hyperactivity, or autism. The teacher hoped the practice would help his students weather the adjustment to middle school. After 12 weeks, the students wrote about their experiences:

"I know it works because when I get mad at my sister, I use it. Trust me, it works really good."

"I was about to take the test. I was very stressed. But I remembered 'S.T.O.P.' When I was done with the positions I was very relaxed."

"Every Saturday I use it for bowling."

"My mom was stressed, so I taught her to 'S.T.O.P.' and that really helped her to calm down."

"I don't know how they did it but they made relaxation work."

For me, this is the point of school yoga practice: empowering students to gracefully handle the stresses of everyday life. The R of relaxation is as vital as reading, 'riting, and 'rithmetic.

For school administrators, the persuasive rationale is that yoga practice improves academic productivity and reduces behaviors that interrupt learning. Schools are accountable for test scores. Recently I asked Principal Scott to approve my letter asking parents for consent. He said, "Write that it will help with the state test, and I'll approve it."

Whether for test-taking or for life, everyone wants students to use their yoga off the mat. Transfer depends on consistent support and follow-through from the adults mentoring the child.

As a school psychologist, I am only in my schools one or two days per week. I teach once a week. Follow-through depends on others. In our original project, Louise taught three times per week. Sally and Daniela provided daily modeling and prompting for the students and their other teachers.

The children in my current situation are in small groups and respond well within the sessions, but do not reliably transfer their self-calming skills. I give their teachers information, posters, prompt cards, and storybooks, but they truly are overwhelmed with responsibilities and lack time to study them or meet with me.

For my classroom sessions, teachers are present. By assisting, they learn to improve their own equilibrium and use voice, expression, and posture to create a more calming classroom environment. They incorporate and reinforce the use of S.T.O.P. This involves a learning curve. Ms. Davis initially viewed my sessions as planning time, wherein she could catch up on paperwork. From her desk, she intermittently called the names of noisy or distracted students, stating that they were being "clipped down" in the classroom's behavior chart. She believed she was helping me, but this interrupted flow and drew attention to behaviors I was ignoring or re-shaping. Beginning the next class, I announced, "Ms. Davis will 'clip up' students who follow instructions quietly." She followed my lead. Quietly circulating among the students, Ms. Davis found those participating most attentively and put stickers on their backs, rather than interrupt their attention to the practice. This was highly effective.

Ms. Davis's room was large. She rearranged furniture to create floor space for yoga and a relaxation corner with an S.T.O.P. poster. She encouraged students to write about S.T.O.P. and Relax in their journals, and they enjoyed reading their entries aloud. Thalia held her temper when her noisy siblings blocked the television. Juan uses S.T.O.P. "so I don't blow my top because that really helps me concentrate on what I have to do at school or at home." When Vernon was disrupting class, Matt told him, "You need to do S.T.O.P."

Students receive the most practice and support when their teachers are the ones leading the instruction. Principal Scott has agreed to support the kindergarten teachers' request to teach S.T.O.P. and Relax themselves, daily, in their classrooms. Their motivation? Many of their incoming students have underdeveloped language and vocabulary. These children are easily frustrated, impulsive, and prone to behavioral outbursts. For next year, expectations for attainment within the kindergarten reading curriculum were raised to levels that challenge the developmental capacity of many five-year-olds. This is a recipe for stress and meltdowns. The teachers believe yoga practice throughout kindergarten will foster students' composure and learning. We will share progress and methods at faculty meetings and parent conferences. The kindergarten staff hopes the teachers of subsequent grades will follow their lead.

School yoga is about more than bringing yoga to children, in the place where they spend the most time. It is about infusing yoga throughout the school and, ultimately, the community. Everyone contributing to the child's learning has the potential to foster equanimity. Establishing school yoga might be a daunting effort, but is definitely a change for the better.

I hope to have another success story to tell next school year.

Andrea's Coda

Here is a personal, descriptive reflection that would easily serve as part of a program self-evaluation. What a different voice we get from this school psychologist than what we might find in a traditional program report. Debra attends to the particular needs of her students, recognizing them as young people who are highly susceptible to stress just by being introduced to an inclusive public schooling environment. She recognizes their body-based tensions from reflecting on her own struggles and the yoga practice that was able to relieve them.

Debra decided not to use the word "yoga" in describing her program. She takes the position that "Efforts to explain that Hatha practice was not religion would waste time and energy." This was a strategic move. Debra is using the discourse of power in public school (Hyde, 2012). Debra looked for evidence—knowing this was the exact political capital needed to support her program with the school administration. She also took advantage of preoccupations with students passing standardized tests. She framed her program in terms of reducing stress and preventing meltdowns so that teachers and students would be more successful in testing.

As Piepmeier, Cantrell, and Maggio (2014) argue, disability is a feminist issue. The fields of Women's Studies and Disabilities Studies both feature advocacy and focus on power and privilege. (Both ability and gender are social constructions.) Students with autism belong to a school population often singled out for study because of their status as behaviorally deviant.

Debra works with Louis Goldberg, who includes several studies in her book (2013), *Yoga Therapy for Children with Autism and Special Needs*. Debra speaks of teaching yoga to her students to support their happiness and relaxation. I read this as an ethical act and her use of yoga here is as an empowering tool for self-regulation and self-calm.

This narrative reports on a yoga program as evidence of its intentions, planning, implementation, adjustments, and results. What the qualitative format also yields is the connection between the teacher(s) and the students (researcher/participants), which is arguably one of the most significant factors in the program's design and outcomes. Here, you have the story of specific people in limited contexts. Others are encouraged to try the S.T.O.P. program for themselves but no claims are made about its generalizability. The assumption is that students, teachers, and school-communities are unique and the work that they do together must be custom-built.

Note

1. *Treatment and Education of Autistic and related Communication Handicapped Children*, University of North Carolina, www.teacch.com.

References

Benson, H. (1976). *The Relaxation Response.* NY: HarperCollins.

Gray, C. (1993). *The Original Social Story Book.* Arlington, TX: Future Horizons, Inc.

Groden, J., Cautela, J. R., & Groden, G. (1989). *Breaking the barriers I: Relaxation techniques for people with special needs* [Video Recording]. Champaign, IL: Research Press.

Groden, J., Cautela, J. R., Prince, S., & Berryman, J. (1994). The impact of stress and anxiety on individuals with autism and developmental disabilities. In E. Schopler & G. B. Mesibov (Eds.), *Behavioral Issues in Autism* (pp. 177–194). New York: Plenum Press.

Goldberg, L. (2004). Creative Relaxation: A Yoga-based program for regular and exceptional student education. *International journal of yoga therapy, 14*(1), 68–78.

Hyde, A. M. (2012). The yoga in schools movement: Using standards for educating the whole child and making space for teacher self-care. In J. A. Gorlewski, B. Porfilio, & D. A. Gorlewski (Eds.), *Using Standards and High-Stakes Testing for Students: Exploiting Power with Critical Pedagogy* (pp. 109–126). New York: Peter Lang Publishing, Inc.

Piepmeier, A., Cantrell, A., & Maggio, A. (2014). Disability is a feminist issue: Bringing together women's and gender studies and disability studies. *Disabilities Studies Quarterly, 34*(2). Retrieved from http://dsq-sds.org/article/view/4252/3592.

5

Achieving and Breathing

The Yoga Journey of a Public School Teacher

LINDSAY MEEKER

For the past twenty years, I have worked in public schools, and I have never thought of a better place to be. I started out teaching special education classes, and then flirted with a principalship. However, teaching little nugget language learners is where I found my sweet spot as an English Language Learner (ELL) educator. When you leave at the end of most days with a bigger smile than the one you came with, you know you're in the right place.

I started my yoga journey with zero exposure or experience. It began as a quest for self-practice and self-love and a chance placement in the right graduate course. Ever since, I have been implementing yoga and mindfulness in my own classroom and sharing this joy with others through coaching teachers, providing workshops, and writing a blog. Let me take you back to where the story began.

Kindergarten to High School: Different Kids, Similar Issues

In 2003, I bounded headfirst into my career, teaching kindergarten students with learning and behavior differences in eastern Iowa. I excitedly shared my first job news, and people would often ask for me to repeat it, or their faces would contort in such ways that you might have thought they had spoiled milk in their cereal. However, I loved the job. I loved making a difference! That moment when a struggling student reads their first page for you is unmatchable. Yet, at the end of the day, I felt that although students were making academic progress, I was only putting out fires on the social-emotional front. I was teaching replacement behaviors for the classroom, but I wasn't giving kids the tools they needed to build social currency for the larger world. The social-emotional management systems I was expected to implement didn't embrace children as loving, thinking, laughing, growing humans.

The next year, I left the energy and giggles of kindergarten to teach quippy, less energetic, high school students in Moline, Illinois. I was excited and nervous all at the same time. I knew going into the year that many of the students I was about to teach were heading into school with adverse experiences to overcome. I had students who were seniors and had passed nothing but physical education thus far. As I looked through the class lists, fellow teachers were pointing out students on probation, some who had been in rehab, and they were giving me the rundown of their reputations. For the first time, I felt underprepared. I have since come to realize that being prepared means having a solid plan and the guts to change it when it's not working. I reminded myself that it takes just one person who cares.

The teenagers I spent the next five years with turned out to be amazing. My resilience and hope would dwindle at times, as I also learned that in U.S. public schools the resources for students with mental health needs and addiction struggles are strikingly limited. I also learned that many systems put in place in high schools are designed for safety and compliance of the masses, and I was working with a demographic of students that didn't fit the system. The kids I worked with had brilliance that didn't show up on a test. I had students who could fix the heater in the classroom. I had students whose artwork blew my mind. I had students who could dance in ways that mesmerized the crowds around them in the courtyard at lunch, but they often felt defeated. They needed a system that had outlets for their big emotions. They struggled for self-regulation. I had students who dropped out because they couldn't navigate the system. Every second felt urgent because it could be the second that I helped change the probable outcome for a kid.

Now that I have developed my own yoga and mindfulness practice and the skills to share that with students, I wish I could go back to the cement-block-walled classroom that smelled like an auto shop and roll out some yoga mats. I would be able to help my high school students to discover themselves, shut off the extra noise, and develop self-love. It would have been perfect for them. The funny thing is, without even knowing about mindfulness in the classroom, we did use calming breathing techniques that I borrowed from Lamaze class (hopefully, if my former students are reading this, they can forgive me for saying that) because I knew we needed something! We did class-building and cooperative-learning exercises that provided opportunities for them to actively participate, coach each other, and open up to each other. I was drawn to mindful practices and democratic ways of educating without knowing they existed.

My classroom physically felt different from some others because of the strategies put in place to build relationships and develop a positive climate, but it was still missing something. I watched wildly talented colleagues have the same struggles. They were putting their hearts and souls into the job, but too many students were slipping through the cracks, just as they did in my classroom. I think the self-awareness that mindfulness practices brings to people could have changed that. The teacher education and training so many of us received was narrowly focused on classroom management "best practices." In reality, that meant ways to track behavior and teach kids how to follow the rules, sometimes even by tricking them into thinking they created the rules (not saying that trickery doesn't have its place).

I am now certain we need to teach kids how to love themselves first, how to solve problems, and how to break the rules when they know it will make the world a better place. We need to focus more on helping students set expectations for themselves and how to breathe through it when the expectations seem too hard. That is how kids defy statistics. Understanding that, I wanted to change the culture of public schools. I felt I had to get into a position of leadership to make that happen.

Leadership, Language Learning, and a Yogic Philosophy of Education

With the goal of becoming a change agent, I entered a Master's degree program in Educational Leadership. During my internship, I spent lots of time observing, note-taking, and assisting leaders of various programs throughout our district. While interning for our Director of English Language Learner Programs, Stephanee Jordan, also the first person to support and fund yoga in Moline EL classrooms, I could see a "problem-tunity." Our elementary language learners (ELs) population was growing and their learning environments needed people with the skills and understanding to help them grow. I noticed that teachers needed more training and so did many of the administrators. I thought to myself, "How can I be a principal if I don't understand one of the most critical needs facing classrooms right now in our district, and possibly the nation?"

I am a sucker for taking on challenges that can make schools better for kids and, to be honest, a sucker for small people who laugh about boogers and hug my legs. So, I headed back to school, well-used backpack in tow, to get my English as a Second Language (ESL) endorsement so that I could be a better principal. About halfway through the program, Stephanee (who had become my hero in education) called to discuss a possible K-5 position in ESL to help develop programs and teach ESL in two buildings that had experienced a quick and vast demographic shift. They had gone from seven ELs to approximately 32 ELs over the course of a year. Currently, Moline serves over 800 ELs who speak 23 different native languages and 900 special education students. Approximately 50% of the population qualifies for free and reduced lunch. Over the past decade, the district made student-empowering shifts. In the EL department alone, they introduced a Dual Language program at Lincoln Irving Elementary School, pioneered Self-Contained Loops for ELs amongst neighboring districts, and developed options for biliteracy in Pre-K through high school! As a district, they also committed to 1-1 Technology for 5th through 12th grades and developed partnerships with companies, such as John Deere, to bring vocational options to students. Looking back, I realize that I was lucky to be working in a school district that emboldens innovation and supports teacher autonomy as I worked through my yoga and mindfulness journey.

As I transitioned to ESL teaching, I started taking a course that would change the way I teach forever, really even the way I live: Philosophy of Education,[1] with Dr. Andrea Hyde. (Seriously? I needed to learn "real stuff," I thought to myself.) I started the class with a *Cosmopolitan* magazine in my backpack, a Starbucks in my hand, and the end goal of an "A" in the course, but with minimal thought or reading, because I didn't have time for that. I felt that as a teacher and a student, I knew what I was doing. Here's the deal though: Personally, I was a stressed-out "hot mess" at the time. Professionally, I was your average over-achieving, feelings-suppressing, rat-race teacher trying to get ahead. I used research-based everything. I went to training after training . . . implement, reflect, revise, repeat.

Enter yoga and the art of caring about other humans (including myself), which happened to be part of Dr. Hyde's scholarship field. I learned about educational theory; I realized qualitative research is "a thing" and that I might not hate research at all. I also learned about social justice, democratic classrooms, and mindfulness and yoga in schools. I learned how to be present. The 15 minutes of class that Dr. Hyde took to have us develop a self-care practice was life-changing for me. I started my new job with a new frame of mind. I worked in bits of mindfulness, starting with belly breathing. The more yoga I was exposed to, the more I began to feel like myself again. I laughed more. I cried less. I got up in the morning and felt ready to take on the day. To this day, without looking at my transcript, I couldn't tell you if I got an A because after a few weeks in the course, it didn't matter anymore. This class, which I didn't think I needed three weeks prior, was full of interesting people and they "filled my bucket" every time class met. I couldn't wait for the "free yoga" before class on campus (also taught by our instructor). Then, something dawned on me. This is it. This is what can forever alter the way we approach teaching and learning. The research was there. It was working in other urban school districts (Berger, Silver & Stein, 2009; Greenberg & Harris, 2011; Lee, et al., 2008; Mendelson et al., 2010). It was going to work in Moline, Illinois, too.

As an ESL educator, I knew that teaching language learners is as much about helping them lower their affective filter (speaking anxiety) as it is about English content. Research continues to support yoga as a tool for lowering anxiety, and after experiencing an emerging self-practice and sharing it with my own children (about 18 months and ten at the time), I could see that in my own life. I also felt strongly that yoga and mindfulness would nurture children from all backgrounds to develop a common ground that builds self-esteem, resilience, and the readiness to learn.

A Mindful Classroom: Delights and Challenges

As I sat on the floor of my new classroom at Jane Addams Elementary School in Moline, painting bookshelves red with yellow daisies, I thought to myself, "This classroom will feel like this bookshelf looks. Kids will be happy here." I decided to fully implement a version of democratic class-rooms including yoga and mindfulness practices (Hyde & LaPrad, 2015). I would commit to a learning space where behavior management was based on growth, mindset, kindness, and collaboration. I would give students a yoga practice they could have for themselves. Kids in my classroom would feel what it means to be present, connected, and empowered. I knew if kids were happy, confident, and ready to learn, the academic gains would happen organically. I started with a commitment to academic and social-emotional learning standards and somehow fitting a mindful practice in each day, such as simple yoga postures, belly breathing, and partner yoga poses.

I started the implementation with priceless, patient mentoring from Dr. Hyde and my self-practice. I dug out all the notes I took in Philosophy of Education (they may still have remnants of Pad Thai on them), and I followed the ideas in a book called *Mindful Teaching and Teaching Mind-fulness* by Deborah Schoeberlein (2011). I knew that self-practice was one of the most important factors in successful implementation of classroom yoga and due to my perfectionist nature, if I was going to do something, I was going to do it right. Actually, yoga has also helped me let go of some of the perfectionism too. It's not about "doing it right"; it's that sticking to a self-practice and self-care routine makes me a better teacher, a better colleague, a better mom, and ultimately a better human.

I set three self-practice goals for myself to keep at the forefront as I brought yoga into my classroom.

- Attend a yoga class twice a week, do yoga with my own kiddos at home, and do a breathing exercise each morning, right after lunch, and each evening.

- Participate in a self-care activity at least once a week. Turns out, this isn't enough. Self-care is an every day gig.

- Read something about mindfulness and yoga once a week. Right now I'm loving *Happy Teachers Change the World* (Hahn & Weare, 2017) and *Best Practices for Yoga in Schools* (Childress & Harper, 2015).

Before I knew it, the next school year had arrived, and I was offered a new challenge. I would be teaching a self-contained ESL loop class. This kindergarten and first-grade class was designed to target students early in their language learning journey, provide high quality services in a language rich environment, while also challenging them with grade-level academic content. The class was comprised of 22 ELs from nine countries, who spoke thirteen beautiful native languages, and celebrated six varied religions that I was aware of, and approximately 30% of the class was newly arrived to the country. On the first day of class, these students came rushing into my classroom with full backpacks and siblings, parents, grandparents, and it got real . . . but fun! After all the commotion had dispersed, it was just our little class, and we were beginning our mindful classroom journey together. We started by creating our class promises and learning tools to facilitate a mindful teaching and learning experience. I taught the students to use "I" statements and we practiced them every time an opportunity came up. We even practiced them in pairs using role-play. I taught them belly breathing; we practiced it every day, several times a day. We learned a few go-to yoga poses and built from there. We did this for quite some time. We were playing, thinking, learning, and yoga-ing our way into the year. The energy in the room was just what I had hoped for!

Then, I let "stuff" get in the way. We would sometimes forget or "put off" yoga. I wouldn't always lead the breathing exercises if we had done a classroom-culture building activity that day. I was second-guessing the time I was spending, even though it was about 5 to 15 minutes a day because I was feeling the genuine academic pressure that looms over teachers of even the youngest learners. "What if I wasn't getting through enough guided reading groups?" "What if I didn't get to the next math unit by fall break?" Little by little I would find myself raising my voice, I would hear kids fighting over center supplies, and the little moments of dis-community started to add up. I was exasperated. "This room is supposed to feel like Daisies!" I thought to myself. As I was talking with the other educators in my room to brainstorm solutions, tears welling up, the dots began to connect . . . "we had slacked on our class practices." We had a class meeting with our students. We talked with the children about how we had not been doing yoga as much and that we needed to revisit our mindful practices and statements. The kids also noticed. One of my little friends said, "My face was feeling angry more." "Mine too," I thought, as his words tugged at my heart.

I needed to make yoga and mindfulness a priority again. I started including mindfulness goals with our posted learning objectives for the day. I assigned a yoga helper as part of our class jobs, who would make sure I didn't forget to do yoga and help lead the exercises. I made all the yoga tools accessible for students to use during free playtime and when they arrived in the morning, including yoga mats and laminated yoga cards that I found online. The rest of the year, we stuck to it. It was still a work in progress, but change was happening. I had fewer referrals than most and visitors would often comment on the positive culture they felt in the room. I could feel a difference in the kids' day-to-day actions.

Here was the cool part: my class made unprecedented growth on their reading levels and our district Math and English Language Arts assessment, with many students outperforming grade-level expectations. The combination of the test scores, positive shifts in behavior data, and the visible successes in classroom culture was the evidence I would need to present this as an initiative to explore in the district and to support the time commitment I had made to mindfulness in my classroom! Better yet, the kids were talking more, writing more, reading to each other, and leading yoga groups during recess. Parents were commenting on positive behaviors that their students were displaying at home. Some of the kids were even teaching yoga to their parents and siblings! Year one of a mindful classroom and yoga was turning out to be quite the triumph. Here are the steps I took to make sure that things got off to a good start and how I helped myself stick to it.

- I held a beginning of the year family meeting about mindful classrooms and how it might look, sound, or feel different than what they had encountered before.

- I sent home a sheet of links that parents could use if they wanted to.

- I included mindfulness in my daily lesson plans and stuck to it.

- The kids were part of the development of class promises; they picked yoga poses, they lead yoga opportunities when they were comfortable, and they helped lead mindful meetings.

- I put natural consequences in place and held students accountable for their behavior in a respectful way.

- The room included student-developed anchor charts to help all of us stay on track.

- I shared our practices with colleagues and stakeholders as part of everyday conversations.

- I ended the year by giving each family a yoga storybook and a set of laminated yoga cards so families would have tools to continue yoga over the summer.

Formal Training in Kids Yoga

That summer, I excitedly packed up my car and drove nine hours to Pittsburgh for training with JoAnne Spence, from Yoga In Schools. I was elated! I spent the week with JoAnne and seven other yogis, not only learning how to implement a curriculum for yoga in elementary schools but how to truly show myself love and kindness, so that I could have that to give back to the people, including little humans, who surround me. The training was also practical, engaging, and fun. I drove back home, full of joy and armed with awesome tools and lessons to use in my classroom! I'm still drawing upon this beautiful training daily. I, of course, still had lessons to plan, laminating to cut, and clip boards to glitter, but when it came to yoga, I was set. I practiced teaching yoga for the rest of the summer, to Girl Scout troops, my own kiddos, and the neighbors.

The next school year we got rolling. As our loop moved into our second year together, I was able to see the magic that happened as the kids developed their own practices. Students owned their behavior. They were engaged in the yoga practice, and they were making connections between yoga and themselves. They would talk about how yoga made them feel strong and made their brain feel good. They were more mindful of others. And I continued to get great feedback from parents. I was hearing their social language change in the classroom, but also on the playground and in the hallways. My heart would swell as I heard them use mindful statements to confront bully behaviors or when I would hear them ask other students having a hard time if they wanted to try yoga in the grass. This is when I realized that while a degree in Educational Leadership was part of my journey, when you give kids the tools to change and outgrow the boxes society has given them, they become the change agents. When they leave your classroom as mindful beings, they will be the ones who can make the biggest impact.

Although I could clearly see and feel the change, it was important for me to understand how students and families were feeling and thinking. I decided to do some informal research to get the kids' and parents' authentic perspectives on how they felt about our classroom mindfulness and yoga journey. For parents, I held an after school round-table discussion (over pizza) and took notes. I had the students write nonfiction mini-books about yoga and their own practice, and I interviewed students individually. The feedback was astounding. As I sat at my desk, the exhaustion from that day just melted away as I read book after book until I had read the whole stack. It was such a sweet reminder to me that children have voices that can give us understanding far beyond what they are often given credit for. Some of my favorite quotes from their writing will probably stick with me forever. "Yoga is for peace, and calmness, and to help your brain think better for the whole day," "my family do yoga and my family like yoga." When I interviewed one second-grade girl, the reaction I received was such an "aha." She was a stoic child and sometimes I wasn't sure she was letting herself feel our class practices. I asked her, "Thinking about the yoga and breathing that we do in our class, would you say it is helpful to you some of the time, most of the time, or never." She paused for a moment, with a quite bewildered look, then looked up at me with a smile and said, "Well, all of the time." Although the "hard" research about the benefits of yoga is out there and continues to grow, what my students had to say still brings tears of joy. The self-love, empowerment, and ability to be present in this busy world that I found for myself had become theirs too. While I intend to do formal research in the field, this unapologetically loose classroom research that I had done was defining for me. I knew that I needed to bring this joy to my community.

Of course, with any implementation, there were moments of struggle to work through. Young learners are brilliant and creative and awesome, but can be squirrely by nature. I had to learn to let go of the image of what yoga in the classroom "should be" and roll with the giggles and bodily noises and kids who didn't always participate. I had to adjust and accept that some students may choose the option to read to themselves over yoga much of the time. At one point, I had come to realize that one of the resting poses I used offended a family's religious beliefs, and

I needed to listen, apologize, and make a change. There were days that things would fall apart and I questioned my methods that were so different from everyone teaching around me. However, the positive outcomes far overshadowed the struggles and hushed my self-doubt.

Teaching Mindfulness in Education and Beyond

I spent my last year with Moline as an ESL Support Teacher in our Dual Language program without a classroom of my own. I took this opportunity to teach yoga in our English/Spanish Dual Language K-1 classrooms each morning to start the learning day. I was scared to leave my own class that I had worked so hard to define. I knew mindfulness is a practice you develop within yourself, and I needed to trust that students would carry on their own practice. I was apprehensive about working with a new student demographic—mostly Mexican students and families living in poverty in what was considered a "tough" neighborhood—because of *my own* real and possible inadequacies. Would I be accepted in this environment as the White lady who doesn't speak Spanish, trying to bring yoga into this school? As an ally and advocate for linguistic and cultural minority families, I knew that I had to examine my own biases and meet my students as individual human beings. I also knew that yoga was not nearly as common a practice among Mexican immigrants or Hispanic Americans, in general (Davidzon, 2012). I knew that most U.S. yogis were upper- or middle-class White women (Murphy, 2014).

I was also concerned about having less control over mindfulness instruction and practice, as I would be spread very thin, across needs and classrooms: just once a week in each of the six classrooms. However, as the year progressed, I would sometimes hear teachers asking students to find their breath as I passed by these classrooms and my heart would skip a beat. Often, I would glance in to see them in tree pose or a partner pose of some type, a sense of optimism coming over me each time.

In my new position, I visited classrooms throughout the day and was called on to help teachers with instructional and emotional-behavioral challenges. When I arrived at classroom doors, most of the students cheered for yoga time. They showed me poses while I was working lunch and recess duty. I was also experimenting with yoga as a Tier II behavior support strategy and used it to help students de-escalate from behavior and/or anxiety events. Most of the time this was successful, but yoga is no silver bullet for any problem. There were times when I would help a child de-escalate an upsetting situation, only to be called back to their classroom five minutes later to find the child in tears with a ripped paper or a broken pencil. Still, as we worked through the year, adding mindfulness in, I would begin to see students in mid-meltdown taking the deep breath without my coaching. Sometimes they would ask me if we could do some yoga. These small shifts to self-practice were important to notice and I wanted to reinforce them. With the help of a generous, Spanish bilingual art teacher and fellow yogi, we began teaching bilingual family yoga classes for parents and their children. Watching parents connecting with their children in this way was just lovely. I could also see that some families had tried yoga before. How exciting!

Throughout this time, I had also been doing in-service presentations, before and after school programs and voluntary community yoga teaching for kids. I continue to present workshops on mindful classrooms to educators by request. Sometimes, Dr. Hyde invites me to co-present at workshops; sometimes I invite her. As I look toward the future, I plan to develop more workshops, share with more teachers, and teach children in my local learning community.

I hope mindfulness continues to spread as I move on to a new phase of my career as a Director of ELs in a new district where I am beginning to cultivate mindfulness in small doses, starting with some instruction in the kindergarten classrooms. I have also begun my dissertation work, focused on building family mindfulness and yoga practices within a school setting. I plan to collect the majority of my data from family focus groups, and I can't wait to see what I learn from them. Beyond that, I intend to start a nonprofit in our local community focused on yoga and mindfulness in schools. And finally, in the near future, parents in the Quad Cities will be able to enroll their preschoolers in "Grow Your Brain Mindful Learning Academy," which I plan to create as my next adventure in love, learning, and yoga.

My journey has evolved beautifully and organically from the evening I sat feet pressed together, focused on my breath, on my pink yoga mat in my Philosophy of Education class. When I think about that moment, I can still smell my lime verbena lotion, feel the bumpy and strangely craveable mat beneath me, and see the blurred toes of my classmates that surrounded me. It was that kind of unforgettable.

Andrea's Coda

As she explains in her narrative, Lindsay is one of my former students and now a colleague and friend. She and I are part of the same small but growing community of yoga-educators in the IL/IA Quad Cities area. Janet and I welcomed her story because it describes school-based yoga program for ESL students. Readers will get the sense of the multiple identities that Lindsay has adopted throughout her career in education, yet she shines brightest in ESL scholarship and practice. Lindsay reflects on her feelings of isolation as a change agent. Then she settles on the realization that her role was not to make the change, but to facilitate a growth process for students as they changed. This does not mean that she or other justice-oriented teachers withdraw from making actual policy and practice changes when at all possible.

From conversations around Paulo Freire (2000/1970) and John Dewey (1966/1916) in our Philosophy of Education class, Lindsay was first inspired to run a democratic classroom with her ESL students; her mission was to humanize their education. Lindsay observes that new teachers are not prepared to relate to students as individual human beings. She says that "we need to teach the kids to love themselves first." With a mindful approach to classroom management and yoga exercises built around literacy and self-love, Lindsay enacts "mindfully democratic" teaching perfectly (Hyde & LaPrad, 2015).

Lindsay writes, "Children have voices that can give us understanding far beyond what they are often given credit for." As so many of the contributors have discovered from being teachers, individuals—including students—are the best informants on their own experiences. This is one of the central arguments for using qualitative research in educational settings. Qualitative researchers develop "theoretical sensitivity" in understanding subjective experiences, in context, using a variety of supporting evidence from those who are particularly well-positioned to observe human events and give commentary (Strauss & Corbin, 1990).

Lindsay notes that typical teacher education programs do not prepare candidates for how to develop their own social emotional competencies nor to teach SEL skills. As a strategic advocate for immigrant and refugee communities, Lindsay was also careful to connect her mindful classroom with the standards by which she and her students were judged. She is another contributor who uses standards for students (Gorlewski, Porfilio

& Gorlewski, 2012). In presentations to local educators, she addresses how to use yoga and mindfulness to meet curriculum goals, assessment targets, and make classroom management easier as well as more loving.

Like many teachers, Lindsay has found the practices of mindfulness and yoga to be soothing to herself and supportive of her teaching ideals. She reveals that personal and professional anxiety made her life a struggle. Yoga is a natural complement to the range of body-based practices that have always been founts of knowledge for women (Belenky et al., 1997). Just like in any mindfulness practice, Lindsay realizes the importance of beginning again. Even as a committed enthusiast, she fell away from her school-based mindfulness practices; but she returned. That cannot have happened just once. It happens to all of us in doing anything that is hard but worthwhile. Public schooling is a constraining system (Hyde, 2007) where the flow of things can sweep you into status quo behaviors. So we begin again. We recognize our guilty and resistant feelings, accept our human imperfection, and recommit.

Note

1. The ESL endorsement courses were taught as part of the Masters in Science in Education program at Western Illinois University.

References

Belenky, M., Clinchy, B., Goldberger, N., & Tarule, J. (1997). *Women's ways of knowing: The development of self, voice, and mind (10th anniversary edition)*. New York: Basic Books.

Berger, D., Silver, E. & Stein, R. (2009). Effects of yoga on inner-city children's well-being: A pilot study. *Child Development Perspectives, 15*(5), 36–42.

Childress, T. M., & Cohen-Harper, J. (Eds.). (2015). *Best practices for yoga in the schools*. Atlanta, GA: Yoga Service Council/Omega.

Davidzon, F. (2012, March 28). Branding yoga for Latinos in the USA. *Elephant Journal*. Retrieved from https://www.elephantjournal.com/2012/03/branding-yoga-for-latinos-in-the-usa-florencia-davidzon/.

Dewey, J. (1966/1916). *Democracy and education: An introduction to the philosophy of education*. New York, NY: Macmillan.

Freire, P. (2000). *Pedagogy of the oppressed (30th anniversary ed.)*. New York, NY: Continuum International Publishing Group. (Original work published 1970).

Gorlewski, J., Porfilio, B., & Gorlewski, D. (Eds.). (2012). *Using standards and high-stakes testing for students: Exploiting power with critical pedagogy.* New York: Peter Lang Publishing, Inc.

Greenberg, M., & Harris, A. (2011). Nurturing mindfulness in children and youth: Current state of research. *Child Development Perspectives, 6*(2), 161–166.

Hahn, T. N., & Weare, K. (2017). *Happy Teachers Change the World.* Berkeley, CA: Parallax Press.

Hyde, A. (2007). Self-constitution as resistance to normalization: Educator agency in the era of accountability. Doctoral Dissertation, University of Pittsburgh, 2007, ETD. http://d-scholarship.pitt.edu/7325/.

Hyde, A. M., & LaPrad, J. G. (2014). Mindfulness, democracy, and education. *Democracy and Education, 23*(2), 1–12.

Lee, L., Semple, R., Rosa, D., & Miller, L. (2014). Mindfulness-based cognitive therapy for children: Results of a pilot study. *Journal of Cognitive Psychotherapy, 22*(1), 15–28.

Mendelson, T., Greenberg, M. T., Dariotis, J. K., Gould, L. F., Rhoades, B. L., & Leaf, P. J. (2010). Feasibility and preliminary outcomes of a school-based mindfulness intervention for urban youth. *Journal of Abnormal Child Psychology, 38*(7), 985–994.

Murphy, R. (2014, July 8). Why your yoga class is so White. *The Atlantic.* Retrieved from https://www.theatlantic.com/national/archive/2014/07/why-your-yoga-class-is-so-white/374002/.

Shoeberlein, D. (2011). *Mindful teaching & teaching mindfulness: A guide for anyone who teaches anything.* Somerville, MA: Wisdom Publications.

Section II

National Programs

6

Empowering Schools from the Inside

Training Leaders for Sustainable Yoga

LISA FLYNN

During a dark period of depression and anorexia in my college years, I was offered yoga as recreation therapy while staying at an in-patient treatment facility. I remember it was quiet; I had to move my body slowly, and focus on my breathing. We were invited to relax and rest at the end. I despised it at first. I wanted to RUN instead, run away from feeling anything, run away from being present in the moment and in the body that I loathed so much, run and run until total exhaustion as I had been doing for more than two years, the pain of starvation and over-exercise much preferred to that of experiencing my emotions. But, of course, that wasn't allowed. They didn't want me burning calories. Besides, they explained, an eating disorder, like alcohol and drug abuse, cutting, or over-exercising, are all insidious modes of self-harm: misguided approaches to self-regulation when coping with unmet wants or needs. And we were there to learn a new way.

During my time at the hospital, I learned about mindful walking, gardening and cooking for nourishment, journaling and sharing with peers and counselors, and then there was the yoga. The yoga practice provided me a way to begin to build self-awareness, to get safely into, and then start to appreciate, the miracle of my physical body. I didn't fully appreciate it while there in the hospital, but the seeds were firmly planted.

Years later, much healthier and deep into a career as a marketing director, I found myself continuing on with some of these mindful practices on my own, which I got more serious about when pregnant with my first child. The more I practiced, the more I was drawn to practice, and the more mindful I became. It wasn't a conscious thing but, over time, those little seeds grew into something that resembled self-compassion. The shame, worthlessness, and self-loathing I had literally starved myself with were slowly replaced with gentleness, kindness, acceptance, forgiveness, and even self-love. It was a new way of thinking and being. I found I was better able to be with difficult emotions, less reactive, easier on myself. At the same time, being more mindful and self-compassionate was becoming easier, safer, and I was more deeply connecting with others. I survived. I was healing.

At some point, I learned that one of my hospital "inmates," as we jokingly called ourselves, just a teen when I knew her, had not been as fortunate. She died when her heart finally gave up, exhausted of the struggle for nourishment that my young friend was unable to provide it. I was devastated . . . and angry.

Why? How does this happen? Can it be prevented? If so, how?

These were the questions I carried with me into adulthood, a career, and marriage. And these same questions hit me square in the face once again when I had children of my own. I began to wonder if having these tools earlier in life may have made a difference. Could yoga serve as preventative "medicine," helping to strengthen emotional resilience, particularly for children and youth who, like me, had been affected by trauma and adverse childhood experiences (ACEs) (Larkin, Shields & Anda, 2012)? Eventually, my anger and frustration morphed into curiosity, and then to determination to find a way to support the health and well-being of my own children, and perhaps others.

Teaching Yoga to Kids

I searched my local area for children and/or family yoga classes to attend with my then infant and toddler but came up empty-handed so I attended the first of dozens of adult and children's yoga teacher trainings in 2003.

My training and the body of supporting evidence, backed by my own personal experiences, convinced me of the immense value of yoga and mindfulness to support trauma recovery, stress management, and emotional resilience. I had found my calling. I officially founded ChildLight Yoga in 2005 and was soon teaching up to 15 classes per week for children and families.

By the time my children started at Central Elementary School in South Berwick, Maine, I was known in my community as the "yoga lady." Almost as soon as school began, I was invited to share yoga in their classrooms as a volunteer. My daughter would proudly demonstrate at the front of the class with me. My son, not quite as keen to share me during my visits, would hide under his desk and scowl out, "Can't you just be a normal mom?" In any case, I was soon to discover that teaching in a school and teaching in a studio provided two very different contexts . . . and opportunities.

Before "going to school," my teaching experience had primarily been limited to opt-in yoga classes typically held at studios, as a preschool special, or as an after school program. I was working mostly with children of middle-class families who already had some awareness and appreciation of the benefits of yoga. But, working in classrooms and schools, where children spend the majority of their time each day, provided an opportunity to reach *all* children, including and especially those with the greatest challenges outside of school, who could potentially benefit the most. I was intrigued by this idea.

It quickly became apparent that what I was sharing in the studio setting was not entirely appropriate for the classroom. There was no space for rolling out yoga mats or taking off shoes in a space-crunched room filled with desks and chairs. Chanting "Om" and putting hands together in front of the heart, even using Sanskrit terms such as "Namaste," could have easily been construed as esoteric at best, religious at worst (Cook-Cottone, Lemish & Guyker, 2017). And, teachers were finding it difficult to fit a traditional 45-minute to 1-hour class with me into their already over-scheduled day. I needed to modify my teaching significantly to be school-appropriate and classroom-friendly.

By all accounts, both anecdotal as well as communicated in pre-, post- and follow-up teacher perception surveys, the school-ready yoga and mindfulness practices I was sharing in the classroom provided the same benefits as a studio class: self-awareness, self-management tools, social skills, improved focus, and behavior. Beyond benefits for individual students, teachers were consistently noting improvements in classroom climate, student engagement in learning, overall learning readiness, and even their own state of being after our sessions (Bogard, 2010). Parents often shared with us how their children were integrating what they had learned outside of school, even years later.

Second/third grade teacher Kathy Bousquet, wrote us a letter to share her thoughts on the many ways that yoga was helping her classroom: "Working through practicing poses and improving, or being able to do something they couldn't previously do, gives children confidence, increases self-esteem and is a reminder that anything we do (reading, writing and math included) improves with practice and discipline." She goes on to say that yoga "supports respecting individual differences as students discover that what is 'easy' for someone may be challenging for someone else." I was particularly pleased to hear that the time they spend on yoga "is not 'lost' academic time (a concern of some teachers). It actually increases student productivity on academic tasks. The children are more focused, alert, better listeners, more able to follow directions, and are more relaxed during challenging tasks" and that "practicing yoga in the classroom helps [her] feel more relaxed." Specifically, she describes being more patient and calm with the children, even during stressful situations.

Yoga4Classrooms

After three years of sharing yoga and mindfulness in the classrooms at Central School, and with valuable feedback from the administrators, educators, the school counselor, the speech therapist, students, and parents, I developed what is now known as Yoga4Classrooms, a classroom-friendly, secular yoga and mindfulness program for schools that supports social, emotional and physical health and wellness, learning readiness, and positive climate, and helps schools meet school goals while giving children skills for academic and life success. This grew into the development of a one-day workshop for educators and other school professionals, a classroom residency program, and the Yoga4Classrooms Activity Card Deck.

In 2011, we partnered with UMass-Lowell and Brigham and Women's Hospital, Harvard Medical School, to conduct the first research study to use both physiological (quantitative) data and teacher self-reports (qualitative data) to examine the acute and longitudinal effects of a school-based yoga intervention in young children (Butzer, et al., 2015). Not surprisingly, the results of our study supported the rest of the growing body of evidence supporting yoga for children and in schools (see Butzer & Flynn, 2017).

We were inspired by the impact we were having in schools and started getting requests for support from schools around the country. At the same time, yoga teachers were asking to join our mission. In my excitement to grow and serve as many schools and children as possible, I decided to scale the program by developing a train-the-trainer license model for yoga teachers. But, there were issues. First, we had hundreds of individual educators, school counselors, and other school professionals attending our public workshops offered around the country, often funding their own attendance. They were inspired to implement what they had learned in their own classrooms and many were having great success. However, we also heard about frustration with the lack of broader support at their schools and the fact that what their students were learning and benefitting from was discontinued when students moved on to the next grade. The typical question was, "How do I gain buy-in and support for schoolwide implementation when I know everyone in my school would benefit?"

Second, when we did have an opportunity to provide an in-service workshop and/or a classroom residency at a school, pre-and post-survey data for students and teachers was tremendously positive. However, when the program ended and we left the building, we found only a handful of teachers were consistently continuing to use the program in their classrooms at our follow-up meetings several months later.

Third, we noticed that though many schools understood the value of yoga and mindfulness education integration, finding funding to provide in-service training and program delivery, including supplies, was almost always a challenge. Funding sources, when there were some, were typically pieced together—some Title I funds here, a few discretionary funds there, some professional development funds, a small local grant, Parent-Teacher Organization fundraising money, etc. It was almost never easy or straightforward, and often took a great deal of effort and time for schools to procure the necessary funding.[1]

Fourth, we also soon realized that each school is entirely unique (even those within the same district), and a cookie-cutter curriculum, no matter how perfectly suited for one school, may not address the varied needs and goals of another. I had developed a beautiful ten session,

30-minute lesson curricula for a typical, middle-class, suburban, mostly White school. Certainly, the base curriculum provided a great starting point, but we realized that individual schools, and even particular classrooms, needed flexibility to adapt the program to their own specific intentions and goals. Was it even appropriate to have a middle-class, white, female external program provider in demographically, culturally and language-diverse schools delivering this curriculum?

Fifth, the ultimate intention of Y4C has always been to inspire and empower teachers to confidently and effectively integrate mindful practices throughout the day, as needed. With just one day of training, this expectation was unrealistic. Clearly, we were missing an important component— long-term support to ensure sustainability. But how could we do that in a way that didn't require already nonexistent funding?

And finally, the yoga teachers who had attended our trainings to become certified school yoga providers were frustrated with the lack of opportunities to share their services in their school communities. At the same time, it was becoming quite clear to me that our most qualified, effective trainers were actually current or former school professionals with real-life experience working in schools. An "aha" moment.

An investigation of these challenges, in combination with real-life piloting of various models of delivery in a diverse group of schools across the country, led me to an important and model-changing conclusion: Empowering schools from the inside is the most effective way to ensure schoolwide implementation and integration, improve program effectiveness and, ultimately, program sustainability. Teaming in schools promotes a collaborative, sustainable intervention. And ongoing costs are minimized as implementation becomes an internal endeavor, eliminating dependence upon external program providers.

The School IMPLEMENT Leader Program

In fact, it was my experience working with one school in particular that became the impetus for the development of our current model of program delivery, the Y4C School IMPLEMENT Leader program, which was designed to help schools sustainably integrate yoga and mindfulness schoolwide. School staff members become IMPLEMENT leaders by receiving special training in how to support schoolwide program maintenance by becoming on-site resources for their school communities. They eventually replace Y4C staff as consultants to their school programs.

Edmunds Elementary[2] is an inner city school in Des Moines, Iowa. The student population is 95% minority (non-Euro-American/White). Students speak thirty different languages and 60% of them are in the process of learning English. Many of the students are refugees from war-torn countries, many live in poverty. In fact, approximately 65% of the school population lives in the subsidized housing project across the street and 98% receive free and reduced lunch. Nearly all can be assumed to have suffered one or potentially many more ACEs in their young lives.

When school principal, Jaynette Rittman, started at Edmunds four years ago, she found that the students were extremely dysregulated despite the behavior intervention systems and social and emotional skill building programs they had in place. Jaynette and her team integrated their existing tools to create a schoolwide system which they titled Edmunds Culture, Climate and Content (EC3). While this created a new framework for schoolwide expectations, such as "Stop-Think-Make a Good Choice," there was still something critical missing. Students were beginning to stop to think, but they were still lacking the actual skills for self-managing and making good (pro-social, school approved) choices. Jaynette's original intention was to help students to learn to self-regulate their emotions and become more mindful of what they were doing.

After investigating the related benefits of integrating yoga and mindfulness at school, Jaynette and her staff decided to train with Y4C. From our very first call during the decision-making and planning process, Jaynette was very clear that she didn't want "just another Band-Aid." She wanted to focus on staff leadership development as a way to ensure sustainable implementation.

With full staff buy-in and internal leadership, our program was integrated twice daily into the schedule and implemented schoolwide with notable results. After just two years, Edmunds Elementary went from having the lowest test scores in the district to an 18.7% increase in 2016, the most significant improvement in the entire district of 61 schools. Office referrals decreased from over 1,000 incidents in 2014 to about 275 incidents in 2016. "And that doesn't happen every day!" Jaynette said. In fact, those results got the attention of the entire district and Jaynette went on to present a districtwide workshop about what she was doing and seeing at Edmunds as a result of EC3 and yoga implementation.

Now, at Edmunds, demonstrations of student leadership have become increasingly common, as well as instances of students applying new skills outside of school during challenging situations. Jaynette has witnessed students offering to help their classmates calm down ("What's your go-to breath today? Let me do it with you"). In their classrooms, students request time for doing specific breathing techniques to center themselves before a test and Jaynette sees students doing the breathing independently all day long. She also notices students using yoga techniques outside of school, at a soccer game or in the midst of sibling squabbles at home.

Staff members have shared that their own well-being, emotional resilience, and effectiveness have been improved. During one of my observation visits, I entered a classroom during the post-lunch and recess transition when ten minutes are dedicated to yoga and mindfulness activities. All the lights in the school are dimmed at this time, soft music is playing (some classrooms even use nature music and video from YouTube projected onto a SmartBoard). In this classroom, students were quietly reflecting on the "Special Place" visualization they had heard earlier in the day, some drawing, some writing. I noted that the teacher was sitting peacefully on her desk. Her eyes were even closed! I went over to her and whisper-commented about how peaceful it was in her room. She looked at me directly and said,

> Yes, this is entirely different than how things used to be. It would take me an hour after lunch to get the kids refocused. Now, this is just what we do, the entire school. It's like hitting a reset button for the students and for me. Honestly, before this, I wasn't even sure I wanted to teach anymore. Thank you.

Needless to say, I had tears in my eyes. Up until that point, I don't think I truly recognized how much schoolwide implementation of these practices could positively affect educators as well as students. Many educators at Edmunds, and others we have trained, have reached out to let us know they've even been inspired to start or deepen their own personal yoga practices.

The schoolwide program generated a feeling of community, connectedness and overall improved relationships and engagement, which made a significantly positive impact on overall school climate. I was especially touched by seeing all the students start their day in the gymnasium with

Jaynette leading a yoga session. When the students leave the gym, there are several teachers individually bending down to be eye to eye with students, touching a shoulder, looking very engaged and interested in each student. They might ask, "Hey Javier, what's your go-to breath going to be today?" Students, even and especially those learning English as a second language, will reply, "My go-to breath today is . . . ," then make the sign for it. When students get to their classroom, their teacher is at the door welcoming each of them. I watched students beaming, and the respect and admiration everyone had for each other was palpable.

Going into a fourth year with Y4C, Jaynette credits the successful implementation of the program to a number of factors, most notably the decision to go schoolwide and to integrate yoga into the daily schedule. In addition, she highlights administration support as being a critical factor as well as staff buy-in and a democratic approach where all stakeholders feel heard. In addition, and perhaps the most important piece, according to Jaynette, is effective and thorough training combined with a team-based, intrinsically motivated approach to curriculum fine-tuning and roll-out. Jaynette and her leadership team of eight (including the school counselor, behavior interventionist, and at least one teacher per grade level) were dedicated to developing a daily, year-long curriculum to support their unique goals and objectives. Finally, she ensured that all staff members had all the support and resources they required including manuals, lesson plans, photocopies and even assigned support staff to help with the Y4C curriculum and fill in when the classroom teacher was absent.

Jaynette used data collection resources already in place at her school which included office referrals, Iowa state assessment scores and the Gallup Student Poll, among others, and reflected often with her staff in weekly and monthly meetings. With the data in hand, along with input regarding implementation challenges and opportunities shared by staff, Jaynette and the IMPLEMENT leadership team review their curricula and implementation plan annually, making adjustments to the plans for the following year roll-out and continuation of the program. With very little external consulting or resources beyond that provided by the initial Y4C in-service workshop and leadership training, Edmunds has quite successfully, sustainably, and affordably implemented yoga and mindfulness schoolwide. In fact, Edmunds's success has inspired at least six other schools in the district to begin their own implementation journeys, with many others following closely behind.

Edmunds's success has garnered attention for Y4C as well as the Edmunds staff. In 2015, Jaynette co-presented a session with us at the National Kids Yoga Conference. In 2017, we were invited to present three sessions, and facilitate a roundtable discussion, at the Des Moines Schools Annual Summit on School Climate and Culture where 2,000 educators from 13 states discussed leadership, climate, culture, diversity, social and emotional learning, resilience and well-being. Jaynette herself has also done several presentations around the district showcasing and sharing the Edmunds experience, and she receives many visitors from other schools who wish to come and observe what the program is all about.

We highly recommend that schools send a team to IMPLEMENT Leader Training as we have seen clearly that a team-based approach to action planning and roll-out is most effective. When choosing a team, we recommend that school administrators think about the "shining stars" combined with key stakeholders in their building—,staff members who are positive, creative, and energetic motivators. Ideally, these folks will already possess a strong belief in the importance of social and emotional learning competencies as the foundation for learning, resilience and healthy, whole-child development, and they most likely have experience with, or a keen interest in, the practice of yoga and mindfulness. A school team might include a building or district administrator, school counselor or social worker, teachers from across grade levels representing general and special education, as well as school support staff (behavior interventionists, occupational therapists, physical therapists, school psychologists, speech/language professionals, etc.). Of course, team size and membership should vary depending on the unique needs and resources of individual schools.

Another lesson learned though my experiences with school-based programs is that, though I may be a gifted translator and creator, and though I have worked in and around schools for 10 years, I have never been a classroom teacher, school counselor, or administrator. Y4C trainers who are themselves current or former school professionals best speak the language and have the understanding of school needs. They are the ones who now conduct the trainings. This is one of the reasons I changed the Y4C model from training yoga teachers to work in schools to focusing on empowering all school personnel (cafeteria workers, janitors, grounds keepers, nurses, aides, etc.) to implement yoga and mindfulness in their own school.

My personal mission has been to figure out a way to ensure that every child has access to the gifts of yoga and mindfulness. After thirteen years, I'm even more convinced that integration of these practices at school is the way to do this. School-based yoga programs have the potential to offer a cost-effective, evidence-based solution to address many of the behavioral and academic challenges faced by schools, while also promoting emotional resilience and positive school climate, key factors in keeping kids in school and preventing mental health disorders. Having closely observed Edmunds' and other inspiring school implementation journeys, as well as having now worked with thousands of school professionals and dozens of schools and districts, it is clear that to me that the recipe for successful implementation of a school-based yoga and mindfulness program is unique to each school and depends on many variables. It is not straightforward or necessarily easy. But, it is also clear that with strong leadership and effective, empowering training and support, sustainable schoolwide implementation is possible.

Andrea's Coda

I met Lisa through a conference call to plan the networking of people and resources for yoga in schools. She was already a friend of Joanne Spence (fellow contributor to this collection), so I knew of the yoga teacher trainings she was doing. I later met her in person at the Kripalu Yoga in Schools Symposium. By then, I had come to think of her as one of the leaders of the yoga in schools movement. In fact, in a chapter called "The Yoga in Schools Movement: Using Standards for Educating Whole Child and Making Space for Teacher Self-Care," I included Yoga4Classrooms as a program that was "wielding policy language in service of transformative projects" (Hyde, 2012, p. 113).

Lisa sees yoga as healing. Like many others, she started sharing yoga with other adults and children in the hopes that it would heal them as well. Lisa is quite candid about her past struggles with her body; her narrative provides further evidence of yoga as a successful treatment of depression, anxiety, and eating disorders (Cook-Cottone, 2015) as well as a therapeutic practice for developing positive body image (Klein & Guest-Jelly, 2014). But some forms of asana practice can also be used as extreme exercise, a way to push the body, to sweat and burn calories (Roff, 2014). As someone who advises others on adopting a self-practice for themselves and their classrooms, I am particularly concerned when I hear women talk about power yoga and hot yoga as a way to punish their bodies.

Lisa recognizes that there are cultural differences among teachers, including yoga teachers, and the children in public schools. And to the degree that those schools are in low-income communities, the divide is greater. She is mindful of her whiteness and asks what business she has teaching kids whose backgrounds and identities are so different from her own. This topic is informed by scholarship from Black (Hines, 2017; Tatum, 1997) and White (Howard, 2006) educators alike who have considered the advantages of having a more diverse teaching force. These scholars also understand that white teachers will need to intentionally learn about and seek to understand African-American, Asian, and Latino children who collectively are the new majority of public school students (Carr, 2016), if they are to serve all children well. Though Lisa does not pursue further thinking in this story about the teacher-student cultural divide, the story of Edmunds Elementary reveals a purposeful strategy of cultural inclusiveness through emphasizing human unity and the inherent worth of all individuals.

Like several contributors to this book, Lisa adjusted her yoga teaching for a secular audience and removed Sanskrit language and images from her school curriculum. As we mentioned in the early parts of this book, "whitewashing" is a concern among the school yoga community and in the Western yoga community at large. For supporters of this approach, like Lisa, secular does not mean that the practices are not spiritual, as spirituality is a domain of human experience, an experience of aliveness and connectedness of mind and body (Flynn & Ebert, 2013). Breathing exercises are the key. The words respiration and spirit share the same origins (Capra, 2002), which is the simplest way to explain a secular view of spirituality. However, because of the association of spirituality with religion, and the concern for ignoring non-Western origins, spirituality and secularity remain contested terms in yoga scholarship.

Lisa concludes that trained educators (current and former) make the best school-yoga teachers. This is an opinion she shares with other contributors, including myself. She writes, "Empowering schools from the inside is the most effective way to ensure schoolwide implementation and integration, improved program effectiveness and, ultimately, program sustainability." What this means—and it may not be obvious as written here—is that eventually, schools will run and continue to modify the programs on their own, making the yoga service providers redundant. It is an attitude so unlike that taken by other educational services companies which rely on schools to be continual customers, who must purchases licenses and upgrades to their products. But it is directly in line with feminist social action through history.

Notes

1. As a modest for-profit organization, we were unable to provide funding ourselves which prompted the eventual development of a list of fundraising suggestions we share with schools.

2. A version of this story was first published in our blog along with a video mini-documentary/case study. See http://www.yoga4classrooms.com/BlogRetrieve. aspx?PostID=1470466&A=SearchResult&SearchID=30768082&ObjectID=1470466 &ObjectType=55.

References

Bogard, J. (2010). What are the perceptions and attitudes of my school community regarding the instruction of yoga in the classroom? Unpublished manuscript. Available at http://www.yoga4classrooms.com/pdf/JennBogard-ActionReseach-Yoga.pdf.

Butzer, B., & Flynn, L. (2017). Research repository: Yoga, meditation and mindfulness for children, adolescents and in schools. Available at http://www.yoga4classrooms.com/supporting-research.

Butzer, B., Day, D., Potts, A., Ryan, C., Coulombe, S., Davies, B., Weidknecht, K., Ebert, M., Flynn, L., & Khalsa, S. B. S. (2015). Effects of a classroom-based yoga intervention on cortisol and behavior in second- and third-grade students: A pilot study. *Journal of Evidence-Based Complementary & Alternative Medicine, 20*(1), 41–49.

Capra, F. (2002). *The hidden connections: Integrating the biological, cognitive and social dimensions of life into a science of sustainability.* New York: Doubleday.

Carr, S. (2016, June 5). Tomorrow's test: America's schools are majority-minority. Now what? *Slate.* Available at http://www.slate.com/articles/life/tomorrows_test/2016/06/american_is_becoming_a_majority_minority_nation_it_s_already_happened_in.html.

Cook-Cottone, C., Lemish, E., & Guyker, W. (2017). Interpretive phenomenological analysis of a lawsuit contending that school-based yoga is religion: A study of school personnel. *International Journal of Yoga Therapy.* Advance online publication. DOI: 10.17761/IJYT2017_Research_Cook_Cottone.

Cook-Cottone, C. P. (2015). *Mindfulness and yoga for embodied self-regulation: A primer for mental health professionals.* New York: Springer Publishing.

Flynn, L., & Ebert, M. (2013, June 6). Yoga in schools promotes spiritual development and it has nothing to do with religion. *Elephant Journal* [Online]. Retrieved from https://www.elephantjournal.com/2013/06/yoga-in-schools-not-religion/.

Hines, M. T. (2017). White teachers, Black students: In the spirit of yes to African American student achievement. Lanham, MD: Rowman & Littlefield

Howard, G. (2006). *We can't teach what we don't know: White teachers, multiracial schools (multicultural education series) 2nd ed.* New York: Teachers College Press.

Hyde, A. M. (2012). The yoga in schools movement: Using standards for educating the whole child and making space for teacher self-care. In J. A. Gorlewski, B. Porfilio, & D. A. Gorlewski (Eds.), *Using Standards and High-Stakes Testing for Students: Exploiting Power with Critical Pedagogy* (pp. 109–126). New York: Peter Lang Publishing, Inc.

Klein, M., & Guest-Jelly, A. (2014). *Yoga and Body Image: 25 Personal Stories About Beauty, Bravery & Loving Your Body.* Woodbury, MN: Llewellyn Publications.

Larkin, H., Shields, J. J., & Anda, R. F. (2012). The health and social consequences of Adverse Childhood Experiences (ACE) across the lifespan: An introduction to prevention and intervention in the community. *Journal of Prevention & Intervention in the Community, 40*(4), 263–270.

Roff, C. (2014, September 8). The Truth About Yoga and Eating Disorders. *Yoga Journal* [online]. Available at https://www.yogajournal.com/lifestyle/truth-yoga-eating-disorders.

Tatum, B. D. (1997). *"Why are all the black kids sitting together in the cafeteria?": And other conversations about race.* New York: Basic Books.

7

SEL, Yoga and Mindfulness

Developing Teacher Competencies

CARLA TANTILLO PHILIBERT WITH PEGGY C. COLLINGS

During my second year teaching high school social studies, I taught an honors level American history class and one "regular track" class. As a good teacher, I would write the lesson plan on the board every day, though intentionally, I did not label it regular or advanced track, as I knew that many of my students had been unfairly tracked since middle school.

With the exception of a few additional papers for the "advanced" groups, I taught almost the same material to both classes each day. One day, Javie, one of those spicy, tell-it-like-it-is kids, said, (loudly enough for the entire class to hear), "I don't know why we have to do all this, man. This is the same stuff Ms. T. teaches the honors kids." Seeing this as a teachable moment and being aware of the structural inequalities of our school's system, I responded (loudly enough for the entire class to hear). "Yes. You bet it is! Why would I teach the material any differently? I know your class is just as smart as the honors level kids. Do you think those kids are smarter than you, Javie? If so, let me know, and I will change what I teach." I looked around for effect. "Anyone think those kids are smarter than you?" No hands went up. One student mumbled, "No. They just have gotten into better classes . . . ever since middle school." I stood there and thought for a second, then posed this question to the group. "Ok. So, what if your class started getting better grades? I give you all the same quizzes. You are all taking the same U.S. Constitution test at the end of the month. Why don't you guys outscore them? You can do it. You just gotta want to."

As a young teacher who did not quite have the tools to identify where I wanted the students to head, at this moment I knew that I wanted to empower my regular track students with the knowledge that they can move their behavior, energy, and emotions from a counterproductive "we aren't smart enough" place to a productive "we can do it" place. This, of course, was rooted in my belief in the power of intrinsic motivation. We had practiced tools like cooperative learning groups and jigsaw to build social awareness. Now we just needed to put them to the test. I realized it wasn't just the power of the goal setting, positive thinking, and visualization exercises themselves; it was looking at how these strategies "held up" in our schools' often culturally biased tracking systems and how I could empower my students to overcome the weight of their negative self-narrative.

From that point on, I taught both classes the exact same curriculum to prepare for the Constitution test at the end of the quarter. This was challenging material, like essay tests using excerpts of majority and dissenting opinions from Craig Ducat's (2003) college-level text, *Constitutional Interpretation*, alongside historical pieces from our grade-level textbook.

I informed the honors students of the challenge, and the scores on these practice exams for the classes were neck-and-neck for the next few weeks. "They can do it, so we can do it, too!" became the call to action of each classroom. At the end of the quarter, the honors class had a 100% passing rate for the Constitution Test, while one student, Isuf, an Albanian immigrant who had been in the United States only five years, failed the test in the regular track class. Instead of ostracizing Isuf or being openly disappointed, his classmates requested that he be given the option to retake the test (at no objection by the honors level students). The students rallied around Isuf, helped him study, and empowered him with the confidence and tools to pass. On the week of the test, I even found students sitting outside my door with flashcards, helping Isuf prepare. When he did pass, it nearly brought a tear to my eye. In fact, typing this now, more than 10 years later, I can still see that look of pride on his and his classmates'faces when he held his 74% high in the air.

I could feel the "magic" of Isuf's situation and its impact on the climate and culture of my classroom, but it took me years of work with

SEL, yoga, and mindfulness practices to understand how my positive and responsive classroom environment created a safe space for my students to be compassionate, present, collaborative, and ready to learn. After all, being present, as much as possible, is the driver behind the practice of yoga and mindfulness. The ability to be present and focused, in the face of the myriad distractions that today's classroom and world provide, empowers students to take control of their own learning. At the time, all caught up in the excitement of my experiment that worked, I did not have the vocabulary to describe the social awareness my students had developed. I was nosing around SEL competencies, but I wasn't there yet.

Mindful Practices and Social Emotional Learning

After a decade in the field, I can now explain what was working. State standards for Social Emotional Learning in Illinois, for example, rest upon three goals: namely, developing self-awareness and regulation, developing social awareness, and responsible decision making. The vehicles we use to arrive at these goals are yoga and mindfulness. Practicing yoga pulls the learner to focus, first on the breath, and then on the oneness with body and mind. Jon Kabat-Zinn (2012) claims, "Too much of the education system orients students toward becoming better thinkers, but there is almost no focus on our capacity to pay attention and cultivate awareness" of self or of the social construct (para. 5). The practices of yoga and mindfulness harness the power of the interpersonal, of being a balanced and present part of the classroom community where who you are and what you do impacts the collective.

My work, and that of my company, Mindful Practices, fuses the social-emotional learning, yoga and mindfulness practices and principles that fuel that spirit of togetherness, the social harmony of the classroom that works. Our facilitators visit schools to lead teachers and students through activities designed to bring self-care, empowerment, and community to all participants. When these activities are repeated and enhanced, they bring a learning readiness, a presence, through mindfulness, to combat the endless challenges outside the classroom, including negative self-beliefs and stereotypes.

Since beginning this work in 2006, I have learned that putting this interpersonal "magic" into a formalized practice can be difficult. For programming to positively impact the climate and culture of the classroom, it must extend beyond simply adopting the SEL, yoga, or mindfulness program to building the capacity of the delivery vehicle: the teacher. Just as we would never hand an educator a calculus book and expect her to be able to teach its content, we cannot hand her an SEL or yoga curriculum and expect her to implement a program effectively without any training.

In my work with schools across the country, I ask classroom teachers to explore the connection between Social-Emotional Learning (SEL), yoga and mindfulness practices that, if implemented faithfully and responsibly, can positively shape the look and feel of their classrooms. From the interpersonal cues found in the "social" part of SEL to one's contribution to the collective energy in yoga and mindfulness practices, an understanding of the balance between the "Self" and the "Social" is of paramount significance. Taking a cue from Charlotte Danielson's *Framework for Teaching* (2011) and working toward "establishing an environment of respect and rapport (Domain 2, 35)," we challenge teachers to examine their own triggers to dysregulate and how they narrate those calming techniques for their students, if they incorporate such techniques.

For example, when teachers reach a tipping point in patience, they can model self-regulation. "I'm beginning to lose patience, so I'm going to take three deep breaths and do a spine twist. Then I'm going to readdress the class. Will you breathe with me? Thanks. Now that we have reset ourselves, let's tackle dividing by fractions a different way, with a fresh perspective." A teacher's transparency in this process of regulation can provide an ongoing how-to model for students when they find themselves reaching tipping points, too.

By "Understanding your students (Domain 1)" we know that the canvas of the classroom must be an emotionally and physically safe place for students to explore the interpersonal nature of the school experience (Illinois SEL Standards, Goal 2). If the teacher has enough self-awareness to take a 45-second break when she needs it, including the class by invitation, then the students may also recognize when they need a break themselves. Teachers can also feel the energy of the class and facilitate a group break. As human beings and educators, it is vital that teachers are willing to step into vulnerability to connect with both their students and themselves and develop not only their interpersonal skills, but their awareness and considerations of personal, social, or cultural differences as well.

This modeling and narrating of self-awareness and strategies for self-regulation are the first two competencies in our framework of four social-emotional competencies. The remaining two competencies, social awareness and the balance of self-efficacy and social harmony, branch out from the self for each individual to find his or her place in the larger group. Now, that group could be the members of a classroom, a yoga class, or even better, those groups could be one and the same. Collective breathing and stretching, with mindfulness, brings cohesion to the community. With time and practice, the interconnectedness and understanding spread, and the students who once could not work together in a small group are finding common ground.

Another benefit of adding yoga and mindfulness to the social-emotional learning in any classroom is a reduction in frequency of off-task behaviors and misbehaviors. By intentionally shifting the focus from "disciplining" students to creating self-reliant learners who are empowered to regulate their behavior via yoga poses, breath work, relaxation, or meditation, students are given the tools to be present and ready to learn. Ross Greene (2014) proposes Collaborative and Proactive Solutions that embrace the power of the social-emotional in resolving behavior problems. Specifically, the adults who are displeased by a child's behaviors that disrupt a classroom (or a family) work together with the student to design solutions, but first they must establish or deepen the emotional connection between or among each other.

The Mindful Practices model focuses on the importance of connecting the Social-Emotional Learning and reflection process with movement and wellness tools, like yoga and mindfulness, to meet the needs of the whole child as often seen in the work published by ASCD (Scherer, 2010). It is in the regular implementation of these practices that we can also cultivate teacher competency by acknowledging the duality of the educator as both learner and practitioner. This innovative technique reframes the way educators approach SEL, making the teachers' development indispensable. That being said, authentic implementation of yoga and mindfulness practices, as well as SEL, means the practitioner is both flexible and present so that she is empowered to be responsive to the immediate contexts of her classroom and sensitive to its members' specific needs.

Developing Teacher Competencies

Frequently, teachers view social-emotional learning as one more requirement on their already jam-packed daily schedule. If that view persists, it is likely that students' social-emotional learning will be so far down on the priority list that it will be wiped out by every field trip, assembly, and bus evacuation drill. We need to shift the mindset to one that values self-care and mindfulness. As the "delivery vehicle" of social-emotional learning, yoga, and mindfulness, teachers need to develop their own SEL competencies. Indeed, despite teachers being fully grown adults, they may not possess SEL skills that they are asked to teach. Nor can we assume that because teachers graduated from a college's School of Education that SEL or mindfulness was part of their teacher preparation training. In most colleges and universities, it is not. "The overwhelming majority (51–100%) of teacher education programs in 49 states did not address any of the five core Students' SEL dimensions" according to a report on pre-service teacher preparation programs conducted for the Collaborative for Academic and Social Emotional Learning (Schonert-Reichl, 2017, 11). Quality professional development for teachers and staff is the responsible first step in implementing any SEL program.

The teacher who does possess this social-emotional competence sets the tone of the classroom by developing supportive and encouraging relationships with [s]tudents, designing lessons that build on student strengths and abilities; establishing and implementing behavioral guidelines in ways that promote intrinsic motivation; coaching students through conflict situations; encouraging cooperation among students; and acting as a role model for respectful and appropriate communication and exhibitions of prosocial behavior (Jennings & Greenberg, 2009).

Clearly, every child deserves a teacher who has social-emotional competence. No parent or school administrator wants children learning self-regulation from someone who hasn't the wherewithal to self-regulate.

Along with in-class facilitation, modeling, and coaching, Mindful Practices staffers lead professional development for teachers that seeks to nurture the social emotional competence of educational leaders and teachers. Mindful Practices's tools like Goal-Setting Post Cards and Yoga Sculpture are organized into an interpersonal, competency-based framework; each activity in our books is labeled SELF or SOCIAL and lists the specific SEL competency it is designed to develop. In teachers' professional development sessions, we lead teachers through a process to first develop their own SEL competency so they are empowered to experience the activities for themselves as learners and then model and narrate life-long SEL practices for their students.

For example, with adult learners and students aged about 10 and older, we like to use an activity called Goal-Setting Postcard. All are given an index card and the following template.

"In the next two weeks, I will (action verb) at (time/day) because (reason). My classmate/colleague (name) will help me reach my goal if I need support. One bad habit or problem I will need to watch out for is (potential problem). I can Be the Solution by (action verb). Signed: _____ date_____, Witnessed: _____ date_____." Students find a Thought Partner to help them copy and complete the card.

On the back of the card, students draw themselves completing their goal, creating the scene of the achievement. Finally, each participant is encouraged to sit with feet flat on the floor, spine straight and eyes closed or gaze fixed on a spot on the floor. The instructor times one minute for participants to silently visualize themselves working toward their goal and making it reality. This activity embodies the personal responsibility to self and community by not only setting one's own goal, but being accountable to a peer to reach it (and vice versa) and supporting him or her in reaching a different goal.

Similarly, our Yoga Sculpture activity builds interconnectedness through a shared practice. Each participant, one at a time, strikes a yoga pose. The first pose is held until the last person joins the sculpture. Each new person joining the sculpture must be in safe contact (knees to toes, shoulders to fingers) with at least one person who is already holding his or her pose. As the last person joins the Yoga Sculpture, the group decides on a title for the human sculpture. Finally, the groups perform their sculptures for each other. This combination of teamwork and non-competitive physical activity fosters community in the classroom.

The experiential nature of these activities allows teachers to go beyond the research or "the why" of SEL to "the how." Many widely used and research-based existing texts or programs for SEL wrongly assume the teacher's SEL competency and neglect the importance of developing teacher competence as the essential first step to introducing SEL into the classroom.

Schools as Inclusive, Interpersonal Systems

As a consultant and trainer, I always recommend that schools divide the SEL, yoga, and mindfulness competency journey into three interrelated and invaluable parts. Beginning with a quick look at the definition and history of SEL, work with teachers to establish a common language for the activities ahead. This will help educators bridge the gap between the process of learning SEL, yoga, and mindfulness practices and the action of implementing these tools with their students. The second piece is to give teachers the space to collaboratively outline an implementation framework around the different SEL, yoga, and mindfulness competencies, like self-awareness. The final phase is practice-based in nature, giving teachers ample time to implement, reflect and share "real-time" examples with colleagues to determine the best practices for the students they serve. Looking in depth at "involving everyone" (Jones, Bouffard & Weissbourd, 2013), this whole process works better if it is not presented from administrators to school personnel and parents as a "done deal"; instead, the staff, including teachers, lunch servers, bus drivers, and even parents all work together to find the necessary bridge between Social-Emotional Learning as a process and the actions that lead to practitioner competency. Then SEL strategies can be implemented with fidelity.

By looking at how feelings and emotions like stress, joy, anger, or compassion frame a teacher's interpersonal school experience, we can look beyond mere content delivery and view the educator's role as a bringer of trust, confidence, creativity, self-efficacy, self-concept, persistence, and well-being (Hattie, 2009). When emotional regulation in the classroom setting is no longer viewed as sides in opposition (the student being the bringer of negative emotion and the teacher being the receiver), our interpersonal need to handle emotions appropriately and share them productively becomes an empowering lifelong learning goal that moves the teacher and students out of a feeling of powerlessness and connects them to community. This reframing empowers teachers and students with permission to no longer view the "need" to practice SEL, yoga, or mindfulness tools as a weakness; instead, these are the practices of connecting with the humanity of education.

Our call to action is to take the adoption of SEL, yoga, and mindfulness programming with the same level of seriousness that we adopt a new reading or math series. In the case of a new math series, teachers would meet in grade level or department teams to familiarize themselves with the materials and ask each other questions. There would be some professional development from the publisher. The district would probably put together its own benchmarks and timetable for whether this math series seems to be working and what further support the teachers may need. All these same steps would be ideal for adopting and adapting any new SEL curriculum, program, or approach, but this is rarely the case.

Peter Senge's (2012) work around schools as systems encourages educators to take their thinking to the larger, whole school scale. For instance, "What can we, as the educators and stakeholders of our school, communicate across and within the system to define it?" School staff, and especially classroom instructors, must be empowered and encouraged to take a wider view. Each teacher has traditionally been in charge of his or her own classroom, but isn't each staff member also responsible for how safe or unsafe the students feel in corridors, lunchrooms, and buses? How can we, as a school community, build teacher competency in a way that not only addresses the needs of our school community, but also empowers our teachers to implement SEL, yoga, and mindfulness? We must encourage them first to focus on their own interpersonal needs. If we expect any schoolwide initiative to have a positive impact on student learning, we must build individual teacher competency and create a program that is not only sustainable but also reflective of the needs of the school in which the classroom is housed.

When my father began his teaching career in the 1970s (coincidentally at the same high school where I began mine thirty years later), there was a smoking room for both students and teachers to access during passing periods. As modern educators, we shudder at the mere idea of teachers modeling smoking for students. Yet, many of us miss the parallel in the ways we model unhealthy coping strategies for dealing with stress, daily, in front of our students. If educators are empowered with the SEL tools to "know better" we should view teachers who "snap" at students and colleagues or use shaming language with same distaste as those that were lighting up cigarettes with students forty years ago. And conversely, we should be compassionate with ourselves if we can't quite achieve the self-actualized model behavior we'd like to display in front of our classroom every day and in every staff meeting.

By providing time for "reflective practice" as in "reflecting in action and reflecting on action" (Hargreaves & Fullan, 2012), teachers and school personnel are now able to identify the times throughout the day when the implementation of SEL, yoga, and mindfulness strategies most benefit themselves and their students so that they are equipped to effectively cope with life's stressors. Whether it is with a yoga pose, a relaxation activity, or a quick meditation break, viewing their daily lessons through the lens of SEL teachers are able to reflect on self, reflect on practices, and create space to mindfully model practices for students.

The positive outcomes of successful SEL, yoga, and mindfulness implementation, namely the creation of a classroom climate and culture that brings educators and students into interpersonal connection, moves teachers from viewing SEL as something that "underperforming" children need as a "special treatment" to a collective learning process and set of skills needed by all. Learning and practicing how to effectively handle stress, be present in challenging situations, understand the body's cues, and regulate emotions, helps us to experience and understand the commonalities shared across age/position, class, gender, and culture for both educator and student alike.

Andrea's Coda

In the time that I first discussed the idea for this project with Carla, her own publishing career took off! She invited her writing partner/editor, Peggy to write the story of Mindful Practices. Carla and I (Andrea) are both Illinois teacher educators in our own ways. We both use the Illinois Professional Teaching Standards to support our emphasis on teacher self-care and SEL professional education for teachers. Carla has been a state leader in "wielding policy language in service of transformative projects" (Hyde, 2012, p. 113) and incorporating the Illinois framework for teacher evaluations into her lessons. She is working the system to help teachers and students to meet the requirements that are presently before them.

Her published workbooks now summarize her vivacious in-person trainings. Readers will notice the details of her lessons but cannot know the high energy and exciting pace of their delivery. Carla and her team are brimming with charisma and enthusiasm. Personality is a huge component of good teaching and school administrators recognize this. That is why Carla and her team are so busy.

Carla is also deeply concerned with equity and recognizes that schools often reproduce social structure (Bowles & Gintis, 1976) (e.g., "culturally biased tracking system") which is discriminatory in favor of dominant groups. However, she is committed to helping children and adults succeed within their school and community environments as they are. She is a realist with an idealist's heart. Though it is undeveloped in this narrative, Carla acknowledges the importance of "cultural competence" in teaching. By this she means knowing and considering students' complete environments outside of school (referring to the ASCD's "whole child"). Carla believes in the transformative power of one. One student or teacher who thrives in a problematic system is one more person who can work to change that system. Carla says that the default school culture is not "interpersonal"; it is not presently oriented toward good social, emotional or physical health. I say that school culture, being externally oriented—controlled, regimented, policed, and standardized—is in conflict with a yogic way of being. It is in conflict with human growth and flourishing. Critical-transformative educators are always working to change the structure of schooling as well as the content, while many of us firmly believe society must change first (Berliner, 2006).

Carla embodies Freire's (1970) notion of humanizing education by maintaining that its purpose should be the health of whole people, but also in her focus on teachers as learners. Like so many of us, she emphasizes skill development and self-care education for teachers before and alongside that of students. Having examined the educational texts meant to support the instruction of SEL, Carla observes that they assume teacher competency or ignore the teacher's needs altogether. She emphasizes teacher self-care as both what they deserve and what will strategically make their jobs easier. She champions meaningful professional development for teachers as whole people, deserving of this attention.

Teachers are typically other-oriented and self-sacrificing, and they are socialized to be that way. From the earliest imagination of the teacher as virtuous virgin, who has given over her life to that of her charges (Tozer, Senese & Violas, 2013), teachers have been judged harshly on the degree of their self-sacrifice and their joyful and thankless commitment to students. This is why some portion of the public is always offended when teachers go on strike. There continues to be something structural about this vision of the teacher as always being in service to others. School yoga leaders are fairly unified in their repositioning of the teacher as worthy of concern.

References

Acedo, C., Opertti, R., Brady, J., & Duncombe, L. (2011). Interregional and regional perspectives on inclusive education: Follow-up of the 48th session of the international conference on education. Paris, France: United Nations Educational, Scientific and Cultural Organization.

Berliner, D. C. (2006). Our impoverished view of education reform. *Teachers College Record, 108*(6), 949–995.

Bowles, S., & Gintis, H. (1976). *Schooling in capitalist America: Educational reform and the contradictions of economic life.* New York: Basic Books.

Collaborative for Academic, Social, and Emotional Learning (CASEL). CASEL.org

Danielson, C., & Chicago Public Schools. (2011). *CPS Framework for Teaching Companion Guide: Version 1.0.* Chicago, IL: CPS.

Ducat, Craig R. (2013). *Constitutional Interpretation.* Belmont, CA: Wadsworth, Cengage Learning.

Freire, P. (1970). *Pedagogy of the oppressed.* New York: Herder and Herder.

Fullan, Michael. (2011). *Change leader: Learning to do what matters most.* San Francisco, CA: Jossey-Bass.

Greene, R. (2014). Lost at school: *Why our kids with behavioral challenges are falling through the cracks and how we can help.* New York: Scribner.

Hargreaves, A., & Fullan, M. (2012). *Professional capital: Transforming teaching in every school.* New York: Teachers College Press.

Hattie, J. (2009). *Visible learning: A synthesis of over 800 meta-analyses relating to achievement.* New York: Routledge.

Illinois State Board of Education (ISBE), SEL Standards. ISBE.state.il.us.

Jennings, P., & Greenberg, M. T. (2009). The prosocial classroom: Teacher social and emotional competence in relation to student and classroom outcomes. *Review of Educational Research, 79*(1), 491–525.

Jones S., Bouffard S., & Weissbourd, R. (2013). Educators' social and emotional skills vital to learning. *Kappan Magazine, 94*(8), 62–65.

Omega Institute. (2012, December 7). Mindfulness in the Modern World: An Interview with Jon Kabat-Zinn [Blog post]. Retrieved from http://www.huffingtonpost.com/omega-institute-for-holistic-studies/jon-kabat-zinn_b_1936784.html.

Scherer, M. (2010). Keeping the whole child healthy and safe: Reflections on best practices in learning, teaching, and leadership. Alexandria, VA: ASCD.

Schonert-Reichl, K., Kitil, M., & Hanson-Peterson, J. (2017). To reach the students, teach the teachers: A national scan of teacher preparation and social and emotional learning. A report prepared for the Collaborative for Academic, Social, and Emotional Learning (CASEL). Vancouver, BC: University of British Columbia.

Senge, P., Cambron-McCabe, N., Lucas, T., Smith, B., Dutton, J., & Kleiner, A. (2012). *Schools that learn: A fifth discipline field book for educators, parents, and everyone who cares about education.* New York: Crown Business.

Siegel, R. (2014). The science of mindfulness: A research-based path to well-being. The Great Courses. Available at http://www.thegreatcourses.com/courses/the-positive-mind-mindfulness-and-the-science-of-happiness.html.

Tantillo, C., & Crowley, E. (2012). *Cooling down your classroom: Using yoga, relaxation and breathing strategies to help students learn to keep their cool.* Chicago, IL: Mindful Practices.

Tozer, S., Senese, G., & Violas, P. (2013). *School and Society: Historical and Contemporary Perspectives*, 7th ed. New York: McGraw-Hill.

8

Creating a Nonviolent World

The CALMING KIDS Story

Dee Marie

If we wish to create lasting peace we must begin with the children.

—Mahatma Gandhi

It is early spring, 2004, and the snow has begun to melt. The wild flowers and prickles of the cactus have just started to peek through the packed snow on the endless hiking trails of the Colorado Rocky Mountains where I live.

I am still wondering why I chose to cancel my day of teaching yoga to put on my business attire and attend a Colorado Medical Society Meeting. Was it divine intervention at play? I was still unaware of how strong the magnet was that pulled me to Denver that day. My life changed forever.

The keynote speaker spoke with tears in her eyes about the school shooting which happened in Colorado on April 20, 1999, five years exactly to the date of this Medical Society meeting. The speaker discussed how her daughter's life was spared, but many of her teenage friends were not. We all listened with lumps in our throats and pain in our hearts about the Columbine school shooting, when 12 students and one teacher died and 21 were wounded.

By the end of elementary school, the average child at age eleven will have seen 8,000 murders and 100,000 other violent acts on television and in the media, according to the American Academy of Pediatrics ("Controlling Media Violence," 2005). How can we expect this not to affect our children? With this much violence observed by children, teens, and adults, it seems to me that violent acts of behavior are now assumed to be the status quo in order to solve problems or communicate. Children are continuing to act out more in schools, with cyber bullying added to the mix (Rigby & Smith, 2011). The National Center on Education Statistics reports that schools consider bullying to be the single most serious disciplinary problem (Christie, 2005).

In 2001, the American Medical Association (AMA) became deeply concerned that school violence was on the rise due to studies showing that violence and bullying were increasing in American schools (Nansel et al., 2001) For many years before this, it was mandatory in Colorado for all school districts to have a violence prevention and anti-bullying unit during the school year (Hullingworth, 2006). Even with violence prevention programs in place, the nightmare of the Columbine shooting still occurred.

It appeared that the current intervention systems were not effective since aggression was continuing in an upward trend (Nansel, 2005). Thus, the appeal at this Medical Society meeting on that beautiful spring day in Denver was to come up with a solution to the ever-expanding problem of school violence.

Suddenly, it was as if I were hit over the head with a magic bolt of lightning. I cannot exactly explain the feeling. It reminded me of the scene in the Disney movie "Cinderella" when the fairy Godmother taps the ragged dress and changes it into a beautiful ball gown: "Bibbity bobbity boo." A chill ran through me. I was supposed to assist this organization with their plea for help. As I felt this shiver run along my spine, I turned to the AMA president of the Boulder, Colorado, chapter and said, "There is an easy answer; all we have to do is teach Ahimsa in school." She said, "Sure, go ahead, what does that mean anyway?" I replied, "It is a yoga term meaning nonviolence toward oneself and others." Easy has not been the word I would use to describe my efforts during the past 13 years.

Early Success

CALMING KIDS was supposed to be introduced in the fall as a unit of yoga education, such as learning about Spain, or whales in the sea, or basketball basics. Yet, when that new school year commenced, approaching schools with the proposal of teaching yoga as a bully-proofing solution was not an overnight success. I had suspected that there might be some doubt, so I reached out to Dr. Grace Wyshak, PhD, a well-published biostatistician, at the Harvard School of Public Health. She advised me on how to design a self-reported, before-and-after survey for students to evaluate whether yoga would be an effective technique. From 2004 through 2007 we implemented a research project at a local Boulder elementary school. After the first round of teaching, Dr. Wyshak called me once the numerical findings were calculated. "What are you doing with these kids? The findings are amazing!" she pronounced with vibrant glee. "Typically in research we are happy with results that are over 50 percent. Your numbers are off the charts!" Examples of our results were a 94% decrease in hitting, an 81% increase in the ability to control anger, an 87% increase in concentration on homework, and a 76% increase in focusing during school assignments. These are just a few of the remarkable outcomes. The official launch of CALMING KIDS (CK): Creating a Non-Violent World happened after obtaining these statistics and was originally designed as a six-week intervention curriculum. The program became part of the national SAVE (Stop America's Violence Everywhere) movement as designated by the American Medical Association Alliance (http://www.amaalliance.org/advocacy-save).

To my pleasant surprise, the 120 4th- and 5th-grade elementary students involved with the study found yoga fun and fascinating. I visited the school for six sessions of yoga over a two- to six-week period. The participants and the teachers gave positive feedback regarding their yoga experience. As typical with yoga for youth, there were some students who fooled around, pushed others over during balance poses, and could not lie still for relaxation. Yet, by the time the six weeks ended each year, the children who found it most difficult to focus expressed how the practices helped them sleep better and feel less fidgety. Several of the smaller boys who often got picked on or bullied reported that their lives were less stressful due to the bully-proofing role-play exercises. A better community had been formed. The buzz quickly got around the school and an after-school class for school staff was born. One student said, I love the

'1,2,3 . . . 1,2,3' breathing we do in yoga. It really relaxes me." What this student was referring to is 1:1 breathing called "Sama Vritti Ujjayi." It is a brain integration practice. One focuses their attention on breathing in for the same length of time as breathing out, and, at the same time counting along quietly inside the mind. One becomes attentive to feeling the breath, which is right-brain activation, and counting the breath, which is left-brain integration (Williams, 2010). This brain balancing Pranayama or breathing meditation is very calming for all ages and abilities. Sama Vritti Ujjayi is a traditional yoga technique. I was not creating yoga for children; I was teaching a classic well-rounded approach to yoga education combined with the traditional conflict resolution approach to bully-proofing education.

Conflict resolution is a process that works with two or more people who are engaged in a disagreement using effective communication techniques and other listening skills to resolve the dispute. Bully-proofing programs look at directing students with language options and skills to help them stand up against negative confrontations. The bully-proofing model also attempts to reach out to the bystanders, or the outside viewers of the conflict, to speak up and support a student who is under verbal or physical attack. It is an effective way to empower community concerns and to engage parents, school staff, and other students to be a part of a bully-proofing partnership. CALMING KIDS utilizes these proven systems of human interaction and adds the yogic element of heightened self-awareness, body language, compassionate speech, and creating a caring community as elegant techniques to counteract the "I am better than you" dynamic.

My absolute favorite story happened one day while checking in with the students regarding whether the CALMING KIDS yoga education had impacted their lives outside of school. A 4th-grade boy quickly raised his hand and said he had been practicing with his grandmother. Often students who practiced their yoga at home usually declared teaching a friend Salutation to the Sun or expressed funny remarks such as doing Downward Dog with their pet dog. All the students in the class were interested and attentive to what this boy was about to tell us regarding teaching his grandmother yoga. "My grandma was yelling at me for no reason. She was out of line with the way she was talking to me 'cuz I had not done anything. I said, 'Grandma, take three deep breaths and then speak.'" This boy had learned one of our CALMING KIDS bully-proofing expressions: "When confrontation arises. Stop (become mindful). Take a firm stance (Tadasana or Mountain pose). Take a deep breath (Pranayama). Then speak." In the CK curriculum we also refer to taking three deep breaths while in challenging yoga poses or to help calm down under stress. Thus, to my joyous surprise, this young man took the yoga and bully-proofing education to a level of understanding that worked. His grandmother quickly became aware that she was venting her anger on him, which was unrelated to what he was doing. He recognized that *her* behavior was not about *him*. This is just one valuable lesson CK teaches. The most remarkable part of this encounter was that children at this age are typically afraid to speak up to an adult. Relating to their peers with confidence takes practice and can be achieved, but challenging an adult's words takes a lot of courage!

Teachers were saying things such as, "The kids are able to sit still and focus so much more on their reading during the days they do yoga." "The students are so much kinder to each other!" The principal stated, "I feel that it has made a difference in our school community and climate with our 4th and 5th graders, in the fact that there have been fewer incidences of behavior (problems) outside and at recess."

Some students reported that they focused on their breathing in bed at night, which helped them fall asleep. Others would happily express that they taught their mom or dad how to calm down after a stressful day with the breathing or relaxation techniques. All these were wonderful signs that the students were integrating the skills into their own lives and also helping to spread the light to their families and friends.

One fourth grader declared that he was often a victim of bullying due to being so much smaller than the other boys. After the six sessions of yoga training and working on his strength, balance, breathing, relaxation, and confident communication, he reported that he was "no longer being picked on at school." He had become more self-assured and was able to stand up for himself under any situation. The opposite situation also happened; one larger boy who was typically the "bully" started getting confronted back about his words and actions. His reaction to this mirroring was that he "did not realize he was being so hurtful" and he actually "wanted to be liked" (aka loved). It was an "aha" moment for this young bully. The effective communication dialogues with his peers gave him an understanding of his previously unconscious actions. He suddenly became more mindful of his words and actions. Along with yoga exercises and relaxation, he softened his demeanor and became kinder toward others.

Challenges

Due to the fantastic feedback from teachers, students, and parents along with the great statistical results from the pilot program, with confidence, enthusiasm, and feeling fully supported, the CALMING KIDS (CK): Creating a Non-Violent World program was born. It was time to help the next generation manage their responses to stress and conflict in their lives.

I began to contact schools. This is when the journey became "not easy!" Thirteen years ago my life was not so much on the computer or online. So my assistant and I began contacting schools directly, sending out packets which contained cover letters, research results and a short documentary video. I had meetings with school teachers, staff, principals, and district administrators. I was offering the program for free. CALMING KIDS is a 501(c)3 nonprofit organization which can seek grants to support this highly effective bully-proofing program. Comments such as, "We have a bully-proofing program in place, no thank you." "Is it working?" I would ask. "Our current program is adequate" or "Our bully-proofing program is OK," or "I'm not sure if it is working but we are not going to change it," were some replies. "CK looks like a great program, but parents will never go for it," was another comment. "So, NO thank you."

A counselor at one of the schools bought several copies of my first book, *YOGA KEEPS ME Calm, Fit & Focused*. She would hand them out to the bullies and during negative confrontations addressed in her office. She loved the 8-page booklet but did not want to recommend the program out of fear of the word "yoga." School staff and parents were just not ready to accept this approach. In many schools there were bully-proofing programs offered. Yet even though they were ineffective, out here in the western United States, there are a lot of fundamentalist Christians. The thought of yoga scared parents and the school districts; they thught that I might be teaching religion!

Every year I contacted the local school district superintendent. No cold calls, emails, nor in-person unannounced show-ups at the office can get you an audience with the superintendent, since the secretary is the filter. Each year the various secretaries would report, "I will let him know about the program." One year, it was, "I will let her know about the program." Male or female made no difference regarding getting through the barriers. Finally, after about five years of contacting superintendent's offices a secretary said, "He is familiar with the program and is not interested." Wow, at least they were paying attention!

At the same time that I was hearing these rejections and experiencing many roadblocks, parents were reaching out to me saying that their child was getting bullied at school and the front office cannot handle it. Due to my website, calmingkids.org, reports were streaming in through emails from parents from all over the country saying that their kids had to change schools due to bullying and that schools and principals were ineffective. How frustrating to hear the cries from parents and, at the same time, be cast off by schools and administrators to embrace this new solution . . . but CALMING KIDS and I plugged along.

Eventually teachers and friends started to offer ideas like, "Maybe you could consider an after-school class." My reaction was emphatic: "No, CALMING KIDS is an in-class approach to yoga education. Students need to learn how to breathe and self-regulate as a subject in the classroom." Ten years ago, that was my stand. Just like with many artists, when there is an ingrained vision of a passion which needs to be expressed, it is hard to see through the collective community's eyes. After-school yoga, even now, looks very different than classroom yoga. Kids are looking for a way to frolic, have fun, and release energy along with some down-time or relaxation. In the school classroom, CALMING KIDS yoga can introduce deeper concepts. Eventually, I had to succumb. It seemed that the only way to get this information to children was to begin after-school yoga classes at my studio at a local elementary school, and to get involved with Girl Scout trainings for badge advancement (stress badge, health badge, exercise badge, fitness badge, etc.).

Then it came: the first big break. A middle school had me sit down with their Board of Directors and they arranged for the CALMING KIDS program to be incorporated into the physical education department for six weeks during the next school year. When the day came, I floated down to the school, high on the expectation to make my dream come true. I was ecstatic about this opportunity to finally spread the light. But alas, there was a new PE teacher hired and someone had forgotten to tell her about this new bully-proofing syllabus. The CALMING KIDS program got cancelled.

New Strategy: Build It and They Will Come

My next strategy, back in 2006, was to start teacher trainings. If I could not go through the front door of the schools, I would go through the back door. Training teachers was very effective because I did not need the school's and district's approval; I just needed to get the information to the teachers. I held workshops in my studio that brought in 20 people without any advertising. Everyone was starved for this information. Preschool through high school teachers showed up, social workers, holistic health practitioners, mental health providers, high risk youth counselors, day care providers, parents, and even teens sat in on my lectures. I kept the information easy to understand and implement. Basic movements and postures were taught, the physiology of breathing was explained, simple relaxation tools and conflict resolution strategies were presented. The only prerequisite to study the CALMING KIDS technique was that you were a yoga teacher or knew how to teach children.

Emails continued to come in nationally and internationally seeking help with teen suicides due to bully bashing, elementary age knife fights, violent date rape, and ADD/ADHD issues. Before this time, CK was planned for the elementary age youth professional. I anticipated that only elementary educators would want to study with me because of the research study which followed upper elementary students for four years. Yet, to my surprise, there was a diverse population who were eager to be trained, all types of school staff, including counselors and educators at various levels. That is why the CK curriculum expanded over the years to cover a syllabus for preschool through high school age students. My favorite quote to describe this CALMING KIDS journey is from the 1989 movie "Field of Dreams," which states, "If you build it, they will come."

Originally, CK teacher training began as a one-day program for a quick continuing education credit. It expanded to two days. Then to two weekends (4 days) and now it is a 5-day Children & Teen Yoga Teacher Certification Program. I have traveled throughout the United States, Mexico, Israel, and the West Bank to teach teachers, students, and parents these valuable yoga skills of relaxation, self-regulation, and effective communication skills. Two of the CK workbooks are translated into Spanish, Japanese, Chinese, and Arabic. In order to serve an even larger audience, the CALMING KIDS elementary age curriculum was launched as an online teacher training in 2014. It took two years to create this high quality online learning module with a virtual education company (Streamlearn.com).

Evolution

Since 2015, I no longer knock on doors; the schools call me. What does that mean and what does CK look like 13 years later?

CALMING KIDS is employed to teach preschool, elementary, and high school teacher continuing education accredited classes. Sometimes they are "in-service" days, which are 2- to 4-hour teacher trainings, and other times I have the honor of training teachers throughout the school year. Family Yoga Nights and Peace Assemblies at the schools and Family Yoga Privates, which are family yoga therapy sessions designed to develop positive group dynamics, are often requested in order to help children, teens, and parents learn how to self-regulate and communicate. I am contacted by principals, parents, and school districts (yes, the districts contact me now) to provide yoga education, relaxation, and communication to various communities. The CK Elementary online teacher training is accessed by interested educators worldwide.

Sometimes, at first, school personnel feel a bit insecure about teaching these techniques. Thus, a CALMING KIDS team of certified yoga professionals has been rallied to go into the schools to instruct classes for students while teachers observe the skills. As of 2017, CK and Streamlearn created short films to be viewed in the classrooms to support teachers in their desire to share these tools with their students. During the school day, the in-class CALMING KIDS curriculum is taught with the approach of yoga education; experiential practice of yoga movements with the application and reasons for relaxation, along with the implementation of yoga techniques needed for self-confident communication.

After-school yoga programs continue to boom locally and nationally, and the CK approach of fun and games for this type of class is a favorite for many children along with the "time in" to relax and "tune in" to focus. The CALMING KIDS after school classes are typically physical education, teamwork activities or games, and a long relaxation for the restoration of children's much-needed energy break after a long school day.

An absolutely fantastic part of my job is the relationship CK has established over many years with teen populations. Each year I am blessed with the task of administering the "yoga final" at two local high schools. These Boulder, Colorado, teenagers elect to study yoga during their normal school day to learn valuable life skills, self-empowerment, and relaxation.

At the end of the year I come in and test their learning application and continue to enhance their understanding of self-regulation. These oral finals typically begin with a question and answer session regarding the students' impression of yoga and what they have learned. Then postures are called out (in English) and students demonstrate the asana to test if they have learned poses and the purpose of the position. Systems of relaxation are offered and students are interviewed about their application of yoga outside of school. Students are asked to describe the practices they like to use during the day and to explain the personal usefulness. Brain integration questions can be offered as well. All of this questioning depends on how much they have learned during the school year.

Teen health and well-being regarding substance abuse is always a concern. Each year I am given the opportunity to teach 500 teens across the country how to use yoga techniques to manage stress, avoid drugs and high-risk behaviors, and encourage an attitude of nonviolence and self-control. Comments from these young adults burst forth, "I feel amazing when I work out and then get relaxed," "I am able to control my anger from these classes." With pride in their voices, they say, "I have been teaching my friends how to breathe when they get tense, it helps them chill." As a teacher and visionary, it does not get much better than this!

And yet it could be better! I still feel there is so much work to do. Even in the past 13 years of teaching yoga in schools there has been a negative shift in students' ability to focus, self-regulate, communicate, and relax. Aggression and bullying are still on the rise. Schools are finally reaching out for programs to help manage these distracted behaviors and emotional health concerns. Mindfulness, yoga practices, focus techniques, and more physical movement in the classrooms are slowly making their way into the daily education system. However, there is still hesitation from school officials and even the educators. Health and wellness budgets for students and teachers continue to get cut or not even entertained.

In order to create a paradigm shift in schools there must be patience and persistence by those of us with a passion for the improvement of education for the next generation. Future programs need to address the exhaustion and overtaxed nervous systems that many children, teens, and adults experience in today's busy world. Studies with adults and children have proven that yoga practices reduce anxiety (Brown & Gerbarg, 2005). Specific yoga research with children also points to improved attention and emotional control (Jensen & Kenney, 2004). Many of the middle and high schools in and around Boulder and Longmont, Colorado, have added mindfulness rooms. These are areas where students can lie down, stretch, and meditate if they need to decompress. Nearly every local elementary school in Boulder offers an after-school yoga option for students. It is a slow process worth every moment of small success. As yoga teachers and mindful educators we CAN make a difference!

Janet's Coda

Dee Marie offers a passionate account of how an idea can flower into a coherent, consistent vision through persistence and flexibility. As with many chapters in this volume, she offers an honest and astute appraisal of the boots-on-the-ground work it takes to bring yoga to schools. For Dee, some of this work meant letting go of certain assumptions she had about what would work and what would not, while still focusing on her belief that yoga practices can serve as an important path to nonviolence.

I was fascinated by how Dee's epiphany concerning the centrality of ahimsa (non-harming) to issues of violence in school came at a medical conference. I have been suspicious of the medical field's focus on dosage and cure of individuals without addressing larger systemic issues that are often at the root of conflict, such as racism, classism, sexism, and heteronormativity. Dee developed a unique combination of yoga practices, including breathing, movement, and self-awareness with conflict resolution techniques that address not just the individual, but her/his relationships with others. She offers narratives of both target and bully, showing how well the practices support self-awareness, which can ultimately lead to revealing one's own needs and how one's actions impact others. This move toward the relational can be an important step to the larger world and the ways we are all implicated in deeply harmful social relations.

Even after documented success, Dee was unable to surmount the multiple barriers to bringing these practices to other districts at first. She believed the only way to bring a consistent message of self-awareness and nonviolence to students was through a carefully designed and sequenced six-week curriculum. School leaders and teachers, mired in the drive toward improving reading and math test scores, no doubt saw little time for this work, even as their own anti-bullying curricula were only nominally effective. It was only when Dee became more flexible and consented to offering after-school classes and teaching teachers the techniques (as opposed to having certified yoga teachers come into classrooms), that schools became more accepting of yoga as an important part of students' experiences and well-being in school. This demonstrates how there are many paths in, and we might need to let go of preconceived notions of how this work can be most effective.

Dee's narrative documents the very real benefits of yoga through testimonies of students and school practitioners. These snippets of dialogue are not just anecdotes. They are raw data that provide insights into how these practices are received and employed in the real world of schools and beyond.

References

Brown, R., & Gerberg, P. (2009). Yoga, breathing, meditation, and longevity. *Annals of the New York Academy of Sciences*, vol. 1172: pp. 54–62.

Christie, K. (2005). STATELINE: Chasing the bullies away. *Phi Delta Kappan*, 86: 10, p. 725.

Childress, T., & Cohen-Harper, J. (Eds.). (2015). *Best practices for yoga in schools*. Atlanta, GA: Yoga Service Council/Omega Publications.

Controlling media violence at home. (2005). *Parents' CLIPBOARD: Elementary level*. The Parents & Reading Committee of the Colorado Council, International Reading Association.

Hullingworth, B. (2006). Boulder County Treasurer Office brochure.

Jensen, P., & Kenny, D. (2004). The effects of yoga on the attention and behavior of boys with attention-deficit/hyperactivity disorder (ADHD). *Journal of Attention Disorders, 7*, 205–216.

Nansel, T. R., Overpeck, M., Pilla, R. S., Suan, W. J., Simons-Morton, B., & Scheidt, P. (2001). Bullying behaviors among U.S. youth: Prevalence and association with psychosocial adjustment. *Journal of the American Medical Association, 285*(16), 2094–2100.

Rigby, K., & Smith, P. (2011). Is school bullying really on the rise? *Social Psychology in Education, 14*, 441–455. DOI: 10.1007/s11218-011-9158-y.

Section III

Working with Marginalized Populations

9

Sharing the Practices with
Urban Elementary Students

MICHELLE BROOK

All 16 fourth grade students entered the yoga room, breathing heavily after their climb up the 4 flights of stairs in their Jersey City school. Dropping coats, lunch bags, taking off shoes and chatting, they find yoga mats. I was seated, waiting and looking out at the beautiful blue sky, puffy swiftly moving clouds, pigeons scattering, all suspended above the city landscape.

"Let's all be seated so we can all see the sky," I instructed, "Let's just look at the sky and clouds and say out loud as we breathe in, LET. As we breathe out, GO."

We repeated this a few times, and then I asked them to say the words silently as they focused on the sky and their breath. The formerly energetic, noisy students were still, quiet, focused, and calm. It was a lovely suspension of time, a cultivated moment of stillness. Sometimes, all it takes is a few breaths while noticing nature that can shift a group dynamic and refocus energy and attention for the better.

☙

For many years I designed and taught preschool nature programs, grade school river ecology lessons, and was a substitute teacher for all grade levels. I first tried yoga in 1998, but began a deeper and committed practice in 2011 after the suicide of my mother, who ended her life with a self-inflicted gunshot to her head. She had struggled with extreme anxiety and depression. The loss left me shocked, grief stricken, and guilt ridden. I felt like I had failed my mother at the deepest level: what was I supposed to do with my life now?

"If you can't be a good example, then you'll just have to be a horrible warning" (Aird, 1973).

I was compelled to practice more yoga to learn how to relax, accept my sorrowful, regretful thoughts, and, most importantly, to learn how to better manage my own stress and anxieties. I understood why my mother had taken her own life; I too had entertained suicidal thoughts at times when I was extremely anxious. I knew that I had to do something to change that deep, ingrained pattern or perhaps I might be in that dark place again, as people would often tell me throughout my life, "Michelle, you are just like your mother."

Yoga has enhanced my strength and flexibility in both mind and body, increasing my self-awareness and ability to manage my emotions. In the past, extreme anxiety would go hand-in-hand with negative self-talk, spiraling a difficult situation or challenge into a tear-filled struggle and nightmare. Gradually, I found that my response to anxiety has shifted profoundly; I can recognize when it happens, notice and accept the physical attributes and the mental stories that lurk within my neuronal connections. An example that comes to mind is the first day I went to Jersey City to begin the program. Being unfamiliar with the area, I could not find a spot to park! I circled around the school a number of times getting more and more anxious. I didn't want to be late, what if I couldn't park? I was already nervous about my first day. I remembered to breathe and focus on what was in my control in the situation, and accepted what was not. I sent a quick text to the school counselor that I was having trouble parking, and then I explored streets further away. I calmly assessed and accepted the situation and limitations, and finally found a parking spot, making it to the school with a few minutes to spare. Whereas extreme fear or anxiety would nearly paralyze me in the past, I know now when to push through these body signals and when they are truly a warning that something is not in my best interests. Physically, I am stronger, fitter, more flexible and self-aware. I know what I am capable of and what areas I need to grow and challenge my body, strength, and balance. In a nutshell, yoga has taught me life-coping skills.

Sharing Yoga with Students

All of these profound life-changing and enhancing benefits made me eager to learn more and to share the knowledge so others could also benefit from the practices, especially the ability to manage stress and anxiety. I could not save my mother from herself, but perhaps I could share the yoga practice, especially with children, to help them build self-confidence and awareness to live happier lives by knowing how to regulate their own emotions. With that mission in mind, I completed a 30-hour certification for teaching kids yoga from Karma Kids Yoga Studio in New York City in 2013. In autumn of 2013, I began teaching kids yoga at a local gym. My classes were playful and energetic, as well as calming and peaceful. There was one preschool girl, sweet and enthusiastic, who especially loved the class. At her school talent show she taught the audience how to do butterfly and tree pose and once shared with me that the best part of the class was "spending time with you." One day the mother of this girl, a school counselor at a Jersey City elementary school, shared her desire to support all her students. "I want to bring yoga to my students," she told me, "school age children seem to be more anxious now than ever before. The pressures of testing, home situations and athletic competition all have been having an effect on the way children interact with each other and cope with stressful situations."

I spent time researching successful curriculums and methods to share yoga in a public school environment. She reached out to her principal for funding and a strategy to initiate the program. The following week, I suggested to her that we could use "Yoga4Classrooms" and provide training to the teachers; it seemed like a great idea and would be sustainable long term.

"No," she said, "The teachers have too much on their plate as it is; I would love for you to bring yoga to our school. Students need to understand that they have many choices on how to cope in a stressful situation besides just reacting."

"Sure, I can do that!" I replied.

In the past, the idea of starting a new endeavor that would touch so many lives and had so many unknown attributes would have overwhelmed and intimidated me. But not this time. This was my opportunity to bring yoga to hundreds of children! I was offered a chance to implement my new life mission! I enrolled and completed a 200-hour yoga certification program at the American Yoga Academy in West Orange, New Jersey, and wrote a proposal to bring yoga to Jersey City for the 2014–2015 school year. Then I waited to hear whether or not I would really get the opportunity.

Finally, in March 2015, the news came that funding was secured! However, the school district required a large liability insurance policy, beyond what traditional yoga teachers have. My husband has a consulting business, Better Health Worldwide, Inc., of which I am the treasurer. The company had the appropriate insurance required, so I became the new Health and Wellness Educator. A trip to the school to sign the final contract made everything official. In April 2015, I began a program to bring yoga to the classroom.

I entered the third-grade classroom, and a wave of energy began to spread across the room, murmurs of "Yoga, Yay!" rippled around the space. The teacher asked the children to get ready for yoga, and quickly they cleared their desks and looked up to me with eager anticipation.

A boy raised his hand, "Can I tell you something?" he asked.

"Of course," I replied.

"I used my breath when I got angry and it really helped." He told me proudly.

"That is great," I smiled at him, "it's great that you remembered to use your breath, sometimes when we get angry we forget to do that!"

The elementary school in the Jersey City Public School District is a Title 1 school, which means at least 40% of the students are enrolled in the free or reduced lunch program. The school contains classes from preschool to grade 5. It is a diverse, racially mixed population approximately 50% Hispanic, 30% Asian, 10% black, and 8% white (GreatSchools. org, 2016). There are four classes per grade, with most classes having around 25 students and each grade having one Gifted and Talented class. I taught in all the third through fifth grade classrooms, including two self-contained classrooms, one for students with behavioral disorders and the other for students with learning disabilities. In addition, I taught a grade-level group of students during a lunchtime yoga club. They were recommended by their teachers as students who might benefit from more practice to help them manage anxiety and cope with difficult situations. If selected, a parental permission slip was sent home. Students were not forced to participate; they had to be willing to join. Every lesson was 30 minutes in length.

How to go about designing, structuring, and presenting the 30-minute lessons? Was there a curriculum I could purchase? What were the most important practices to share with these young learners? Where do I begin? These were some of the questions I asked myself once I had the contract in place.

The Yoga4Classrooms programming was appealing. They had a card deck which contained yoga practices broken into several categories, "Let's Breathe, At Your Desk, Stand Strong, Loosen Up, Be Well, and Imagination Vacation" (Flynn, 2014). They sold their cards without requiring expensive training, so I purchased two sets, one for me and one as a gift for the school counselor. I also discovered the Niroga Institute, which had developed a detailed, extensive curriculum and was regarded as exemplary in the area of yoga education. The curriculum was divided into four units entitled "The Stress Response, Physical and Emotional Awareness, Self-Regulation, and Healthy Relationships" (Niroga, 2012). I was able to obtain a copy by taking their online training for $150; an investment I felt was worth the cost, even though the program is geared to middle school and high school students. I began to adapt the two programs into classroom lessons for the elementary students, using the thematic units and select lessons from Niroga as the topics for each lesson. These topics included the stress response, calming yourself, recognizing stress, centering yourself, focusing attention, and healthy relationships. Using these topics, along with the breathing practices, desk poses, standing poses, and guided imagery as described in the card deck from Yoga4Classrooms, my 30-minute lessons were created. The overall goals for the program were to provide practices and tools for handling stress and strong emotions, helping to focus attention, and learning to self-regulate and control responses. My classroom lessons contained an introduction to the topic, an opening routine, breathwork, seated and standing poses, and guided relaxation, and ended with a topic review and closing routine.

Another consideration in beginning this public school program was to avoid potential conflicts with parents perceiving yoga as a "religious" practice. I had the permission of the administration to use the word "Om" at the beginning of the class to join our voices together. (Recently, I have become uncomfortable using "Om" as I am aware of its spiritual definitions, and I am switching to "peace" and/or changing the opening song to address possible concerns.) The other Sanskrit word I use, and confirmed in advance with the school, is "Namaste," to acknowledge that we are all special and want to be happy and free from suffering. In India today it is a traditional greeting of respect.

For the yoga club instruction, I had more freedom to teach a traditional yoga class using mats in a large, relatively open space. I had a general outline for the practice for each day, but I felt free to change activities, poses or breath work depending on the energy, needs, and requests of the students. In the short 30 minutes, often shorter due to the logistics of moving the students from lunch to the yoga club space, we generally had an opening song, quiet breath work, warm-up poses, standing poses, sometime partner poses, and concluding with gentle movement on their backs and relaxation. As much planning as I did, I found that some of the best lessons happened naturally, as needed in the moment.

When I arrived in Jersey City one Friday morning, I was informed that the fifth grade gifted class was full of very anxious students due to an important exam the next day that would determine which middle school they would attend. Jersey City has several middle schools and some are very competitive to gain admission. They were all worrying about the exam and their futures.

"Hello," I greeted them, "I hear everyone is feeling stressed about the big test tomorrow?"

I have a plan every time I enter a classroom, but which lesson would best support this group on this particular day? Every teacher knows that sometimes you have to let go of what you prepare to give the students what they need in that moment. How could I best serve these young achievers?

"We waste a lot of time in our lives worrying about the future," I began, "Let's be here right now. Everything is fine, you are safe in this classroom surrounded by your friends and caring teachers. You are all very smart, capable, and high-achieving students so there is no reason to believe that you will not do well tomorrow. The best thing for you to do is focus on each moment you have and do the best you can with that moment. Let's take some time today to really breathe and relax. We always have our breath to help us find some relief from what may stress our bodies."

I proceeded to guide the students, and their participating teacher, through deep, three-part breath. They had one hand on their belly and the other on their heart, relaxing and breathing into their bellies, expanding their rib cages, and filling their lungs all the way up to their heart space. Then they were guided to exhale in the opposite order, from heart, rib cage and belly. I urged them to focus all their attention on the sensation of this breath, the slow, deliberate inhalation and exhalation. We stayed with this breathing pattern for an extended time, giving their parasympathetic nervous system plenty of time to respond and send signals of relaxation throughout their bodies.

As I gently asked them to open their eyes, I looked around the room. I sensed how they must be feeling, based on my own slowed down, relaxed body sensations.

"You always have the power to relax your body like this," I emphasized, "if you find yourself getting lost or confused during your test tomorrow, take some deep breaths like we just did."

The next time I visited these students, many were eager to share that the test was "easy" and some had used deep breathing techniques during the testing day, especially before the exam began.

When I was a young girl, my dad taught me that the actions we take and the decisions we make can have both positive and negatives outcomes. I recall making lists of the positives and negatives when there was a big choice I had to make and it was difficult to decide. Sometimes it is obvious that there are more potential negatives and our choice is easy. Other times we have to acknowledge that the choice could go either way, and we have to decide with our gut instinct. Occasionally, we don't even have to make the list because the overall positive benefits are overwhelming. I believe this applies to providing instruction of yoga in public schools. Most students enjoyed participating in yoga lessons, the movement, breathing, and relaxation techniques. As they enjoy what they are doing, they are learning and being exposed to coping skills for life. If you asked most students, they would agree.

All of the Jersey City students took a survey at the end of the 2014–2015 school year so the administration and I could assess the program. A total 299 students responded to the survey conducted online with Google Forms. On a scale of 1 to 5 on how much they felt the yoga programming benefited them, 73% selected 4 or 5, 26.1% and 47.2%, respectively. At least 95% of the students understood that the best action they can take when they are stressed is "several slow deep breaths." From a list of various feelings, students were asked to select how they felt after a yoga class. The most popular responses were calm (77%) and relaxed (78%). Finally, 89% reported that they had used a calming breath since the yoga lessons and the same percentage would like to have more yoga in school.

Challenges of Working in Schools

Like any physical activity, such as playing outside or taking a gym class, there is risk of a physical injury in yoga. If there are students who suffer from mental disorders or trauma, we need to be aware that discussions about stress, thoughts, and emotions might trigger unintended responses. There are also challenging students and situations that may arise while attempting to provide yoga instruction.

The students I find most challenging are those with special needs who have difficulty controlling their actions, and students who are defiant and disrespectful. To a lesser degree, I find that students who are not open to the practices and are unwilling or extremely reluctant to participate also present challenges. While I do feel the overall result of yoga in public schools is positive, there are difficulties that must be acknowledged in attempting to serve all populations.

The "Last Class" of the Day

While I looked forward to my teaching days at the school, there was one class I didn't find a pleasure. It was the last class, right before dismissal, the end of a long day of learning and doing. There also seemed to be an environment of disrespect that I hadn't found in any other classroom, a combination of students that cultivated a challenging climate.

My second visit to them was probably the hardest, especially when all of the other lessons were so well received with few or no behavioral problems. As I entered the classroom there was a sense of disorder and unhappiness. Throughout the lesson many students were disrespectful, interrupting and not really trying. Some would be reading or doing homework as I was teaching and I was uncertain of whether I should be "making" them participate. The teacher scolded them at the end saying that maybe I should not return the following week, which didn't seem the right option to me.

Taking advice from *Best Practices for Yoga in Schools*, I was motivated to really reflect on what happened. I was feeling hurt, insulted, and disrespected, but had no idea what else had occurred in their school day. The teacher had turned over responsibility of the class to me, and had been busy with work at her desk. Most students were giving up easily on poses and they also seemed to take every opportunity to be extra noisy, chatty, and breathing with exaggeration. I was going to have to adjust my expectations for the class, give them strict structure and perhaps a longer period to relax. I also sought advice from the school counselor. We both felt that not returning was not an option, and that all students should be participating and definitely not engaged in other activities.

In subsequent classes I had to stress that yoga was not optional, it was part of their school day and they were expected to participate to the best of their ability. I knew if I gave them the choice to not join in, almost the whole class would "check out." I had to take extra time in this class to walk around the classroom, asking that they find "seated mountain" a seated pose where feet were flat on the floor, knees over ankles, sitting up tall without using the backrest, hands on lap. It felt so strange to do this, because other classes would just all sit in that pose when I asked. Everything in this last class seemed like a contest, a test of my own ability to stay in balance of my emotions and reactions, to best try to inspire and motivate them to try the practices, to see what might work for them.

As a visitor, a part-time teacher of yoga to these students, I don't know which of the practices or "seeds" I shared will stay with them, take root and grow, if any. Like any skill, the tools of yoga need to be practiced to become a healthy habit. Did anyone in this class benefit from my lessons? I was pleasantly surprised when a student raised his hand to share with me, about midway through the year, "I use balloon breath to calm down and to focus on myself when there is a lot going on." He followed up with, "How can I join the yoga club?"

When sharing yoga practices with challenging students it is so important to have structure, rules, and guidelines. Within the structure, keep introducing new practices and poses, encourage participation, keep an open mind, and just keep "trying" because you never know what may be helpful to them. Maintain the tricky balance of letting students be their true selves, while keeping the space safe, calm, respectful, and productive. We must keep our own emotions and frustrations in balance and stop ourselves from reacting with anger or overreacting, but still remain true to ourselves. We need to share when we feel annoyed or angry and model the behavior we are trying to teach, such as pausing, breathing, and releasing tension with movement, in order to refocus and move on.

Educating each class, with challenges and without, provides students with a long list of potential positives to be gained, such as calmness, well-being, strength, self-awareness, emotional regulation, body awareness, and compassion. To quote a third grade yoga student, "I enjoy yoga; it helps me feel calm when I am stressed out especially when I do balloon breathing."

Yoga Practices as Life Skills

In Jersey City, there were only two students, out of about 350, who had concerns about the spiritual aspects of yoga. One student left the classroom when I taught, and the other remained but did not actively participate. The teacher with the student who had to leave tried to talk to the parent to ease concerns, but the parent simply said, "No yoga, yoga bad." Perhaps there is a language barrier? I would love to have a dialog with the parent, but did not have the opportunity. It is very important to understand this perspective in order to properly address the concerns that some may have.

A yoga program in a school has to be sensitive to this issue and, I believe, move away from using Sanskrit words, including "yoga." The focus should be on the elements of programming that stresses one of learning lifelong coping skills of self-awareness, emotional regulation, focused concentration, relaxation, and taking care of the physical body. Some yoga teachers would agree with me and insist that what is taught in public schools is not really "yoga." They believe that "true yoga" incorporates the idea of the union of body, mind, and spirit—that we are spiritual beings and part of a greater universal divine spiritual energy.

While I find this spiritual aspect of yoga meaningful, I do not feel that my public school students are somehow getting "lesser" yoga than those I teach at a yoga studio, where I have freedom to share more spiritual yoga philosophy. Keeping the content at school with a focus on the mindfulness of the practices, mind-body connection, utilizing the power of breath, movement, imagination, and nonjudgmental awareness to focus attention and manage our emotions, are very powerful practices in life-coping skills that don't require the notion of universal spiritual energy or spirit.

It is interesting to note that the State of New Jersey Department of Education (NJDOE) defines Wellness as "a positive state of wellbeing in which a person makes decisions that lead to a healthy and physically active lifestyle. This includes an understanding of the healthy mind, body, and spirit" (NJDOE, 2014). Although "spirit" is not defined, it is used in the state standards!

School Culture

The school culture must support the goals of a yoga program, from the parents, students, support staff, teachers, and school administration, up through the superintendent and school board and even beyond. The support must then translate into adequate time and funding.

To begin a school program, based on my experience and those of my peers, it usually starts with an idea champion; in my school it was the school counselor. Unless there are new curriculum standards requiring mindfulness practices, such as yoga, as part of the overall health education, then someone at the school or within the local community has to make it happen. Then it has to be supported by all the people involved in that school community.

One day in February 2016, the principal announced in the morning that there would be parents visiting the school throughout the day, especially parents who had young children who might be attending the school in the future.

As I was traveling down the hallway with my singing bowl and lesson plan, I passed the principal who was leading a tour with two young parents. He was chatting to them as I came along and began to pass them.

"Good morning," I greeted, "I'm yoga!" I announced with a smile.

They turned and smiled at me, I could swear their eyebrows rose up a little too, "Oh, you have yoga here?" They looked back at the principal.

"Yes," he proudly answered, "We find it's helpful for the students for them to concentrate and relax before exams, so they can achieve more . . ."

There was a sense of the parents being impressed and the principal being proud to share that yoga is part of the school programming.

There is increasing support for yoga programming at the highest levels in the school community, such as state government. One day, I entered the guidance office and the counselor greeted me with big news for the school. They had recently been in the press for winning a $5,000 grant from the State Department of Agriculture to help purchase gym equipment and cafeteria tables to provide additional fitness and healthy eating opportunities for the students. The grant required that innovative programming already be in place, and she used the yoga program as an example. The symbolic check was given by New York Jets football player Jeremy Ross, and the yoga program was highlighted as one reason the school was awarded the grant.

I returned to the elementary school after not being there for two months. Throughout the month of February and half of March, 2016, I was a presence almost every Thursday and Friday, visiting the third, fourth, and fifth grade classrooms, as well as seeing yoga club participants for lunchtime yoga with yoga mats. Then spring break intruded, followed by almost a month of standardized testing, creating a gap in the programming.

Time and Resources

The time and resource commitment is not overwhelming. It costs about $270 per day ($45/hour) to bring a yoga instructor, specially trained in kids yoga, to the school. In one day they can provide 8 or 9 half-hour yoga lessons throughout the school population. For a budget just under $5,000 a school can provide 18 days of programming, or 162 half-hour yoga lessons! The teachers in Jersey City have all been happy and willing to provide a half-hour of their lesson time once a week. This is one method of bringing the practices to students.

In the future, will physical education teachers have a new requirement in their undergraduate education to become a registered yoga teacher or registered children's yoga teacher? Will school districts have a budget line item for health and wellness that could include contracting a kids yoga professional to provide programming as another "special" in their day? Can teachers with a yoga practice obtain adequate training to become their school's designated yoga teacher on a part-time basis? There are many options available to explore.

"Why did you desert us?" asked a fifth grade classroom yoga student with a smile, when I returned after a gap in the programming during the state testing.

"When Michelle enters our classroom and begins to speak, I feel the stress level come down immediately," shared a third grade teacher with the school counselor, "but then as soon as she leaves it comes right back!"

There is a need for teaching stress reduction skills to students *and* teachers. The skills need to be practiced, like any other skill, for the practitioner to become good at it. Although it won't make the stressors magically "go away," it can help to manage them better. Yoga in public school is becoming not a question of "why?" anymore: we know why; there are many benefits of the practices. It is a question of "how?" How do we get the practices successfully integrated in our school, our district, our county, our state, our country and our world?

Last words and a sweet moment from Jersey City students . . .

One afternoon I was walking down the hallway and passing by a group of third grade students gathering outside of their class. Many of the young girls were so happy to see me that they spontaneously came over and hugged me.

"I didn't know we had yoga today, I'm glad because we have a bench-mark test later."

"I showed my mom balloon breath."

"I got angry and used ocean breath and it helped."

"Thank you."

Janet's Coda

Michelle's journey to teaching yoga in schools originates in a deeply personal and painful place. Her mother's suicide and her own anxiety encouraged her to take up yoga in a serious way, and as she realized yoga's benefits, to share those practices with others, especially low-income students of color. In this chapter, Michelle's personal experiences serve as a catalyst, illuminating the devotion, commitment, and generosity she brings to this work.

In describing the process of how she came to teach yoga in schools, Michelle demonstrates both the serendipitous and the demanding. It was a chance interaction with a savvy school counselor that started the jour-ney, but after that, it was all building an infrastructure through research of effective yoga programs in schools, making connections with school personnel, finding funding, and becoming a presence that children could trust. This all took place within the spectacularly challenging environment of urban schools, where resources are scarce, teachers are pressured to teach to standards and tests without regard for individual student needs or lived experiences, and student worth is measured by test scores (Ravitch, 2010). One of the things I most admire about Michelle is her meticulous preparation and research prior to teaching, and her willingness to stand her ground once she got there.

Yoga-in-school advocates insist that yoga can support students as they encounter the demands of today's public schools (Butzer, Bury, Telles, & Khalsa, 2016). However, as a critical scholar, I also see how yoga is implicated as a tool for student compliance rather than liberation in the highly controlled environments resulting from neoliberal educational policies. In addition, as Berila notes, yoga and mindfulness are marketed as "silver bullets" (2016, p. 1) to counteract social problems, but instead, often end up re-inscribing them. The commercial aspects of yoga ignore its inclusivity by targeting a specific social class and body type, leaving out large groups, including the children whom Michelle teaches.

Although yoga in schools may not lead to systemic change, it does offer students positive ways to mitigate systemic pressures, as Michelle shows through the snapshots (Lane, 2015) sprinkled throughout the chapter. The children's voices show pride in their learning and how they have taken the practices into their lives outside of school. Their understanding of the portability and applicability of yoga offers insight into their deepening self-awareness, and perhaps, a sense of control over their emotions and bodies. This is powerful. This is power.

One of the purposes of this book is to share the systemic challenges that yoga teachers encounter when offering yoga in schools. Andrea and I wanted yoga teachers and service providers to know that they are not alone in dealing with reluctant and/or busy school leaders and teachers, stressful environments, and students who reject yoga for whatever reason. In choosing to deal with this rejection by modeling how to handle problematic situations, Michelle offers students alternatives to angry reactivity: pausing and breathing with deliberation. These are useful practices to deal with personal and systemic issues, especially for children, who, based on age alone, have little control over their lives.

Michelle's narrative shows the complexity of being an effective yoga teacher whose main concern is children's well-being, even as she must navigate the multiple and sometimes contested priorities of school personnel and policies. Even as a clear yoga advocate ("I am yoga!") she is not afraid to show the limitations of yoga to mitigate systemic stresses, as when a counselor notes that the students' stress level heightens after Michelle's yoga class is over. This chapter, like many of the others in this volume, speaks to the tensions inherent in attempting to adapt an ancient system to modern structures.

References

Aird, C. (1973). *His Burial Too*. Quote from Author. Retrieved from: http://www.catherineaird.com/.

Berila, B. (2016). Introduction: What's the link between feminism and yoga? In B. Berila, M. Klein, C. Jackson Roberts (Eds.). *Yoga, the body and embodied social change*. Lanham, MD: Lexington Books.

Butzer, B., Bury, D., Telles, S., & Khalsa, S. B. (2016). Implementing yoga within the school curriculum: A scientific rationale for improving social-emotional learning and positive student outcomes. *Journal of Children's Services, 11*(1), pp. 3–24.

Capodice, N. Letter from principal to parents, 4/14/2015.

Childress, T., & Cohen-Harper, J. (Eds.). (2015). *Best practices for yoga in schools*. Atlanta, GA: Yoga Service Council/Omega Publications.

Flynn, L. (2014). *Yoga4Classrooms tools for learning, lessons for life*, 3rd ed. Sanford, ME. Edison Press.

GreatSchools.org. (2016). [Pie chart and graph depicting Student Diversity June 7, 2016], Jotham W. Wakeman No. 6 Elementary School, Students. Retrieved from https://www.greatschools.org/new-jersey/jersey-city/908-Jotham-W.-Wakeman-No.-6-Elementary-School/.

Lane, B. (2015). *After the end: Teaching and learning creative revision*, 2nd ed. Portsmouth, NH: Heinemann.

Niroga Institute. (2012). Transformative Life Skills (TLS) Program and Curriculum. Oakland, CA.

State of New Jersey Department of Education. (2016). New Jersey Core Curriculum Content Standards for Comprehensive Health and Physical Education (2014 Standards). Retrieved from www.nj.us/education/cccs/2014/chpe/.

10

Yoga for Health and
Physical Education (and More)

JOANNE SPENCE

Yoga In Schools (YIS) is a 501(c)(3) organization that provides yoga programming and teacher training in several school districts primarily within the Pittsburgh, Pennsylvania, area. YIS was founded in 2005 after a principal from a local inner-city charter school called me to find out if I could teach yoga as Physical Education (PE) at her school. At that time, I owned a yoga studio and offered four or five children's yoga classes per week in addition to regular adult yoga classes. I figured that teaching yoga in schools was a great idea and said, "why not?"

However, the story of my personal yoga journey commenced with a life-changing incident that happened several years before that phone call. I was in a car accident that caused soft-tissue injuries to my spine and severe trauma to my knee, which required two surgeries. I spent several days in the hospital and the next two years in pain. During that time, rehabilitation and eventual healing occurred very slowly.

Two years into my healing process, I participated in a weekend yoga workshop. At the time, I was working as a water aerobics instructor at a large fitness club. I had no background or even frame-of-reference for what "yoga" was, which admittedly is an unusual prerequisite for becoming a yoga teacher. At the time, taking the yoga training seemed logical to me because the club needed yoga teachers to meet the demands of its clients. Incredibly, three days after that first yoga workshop, I was pain-free for the first time since the accident. Little did I realize that I was at the beginning of a life-altering journey of discovering a body-based therapy that is infinitely adaptable and has the potential to heal the body and the mind in so many ways.

YIS Origin Story

Back to the story of teaching yoga as PE. When the principal called, I thought that perhaps she somehow knew of my past work with at-risk youth as a social worker and that my life was on a new trajectory now that I had experienced yoga. But, no, she simply had looked in the Yellow Pages (yes, in 2004, we still advertised in the Yellow Pages). Apparently, of all the six yoga teachers listed at the time, I was the only one who taught children's yoga. The ad did not have the desired effect in bringing more children to my yoga studio but, if all it did was connect this principal to me, then it was a hundred bucks well spent!

Working in the school environment over the next few months led me to ponder several questions:

- Were there external monies available to support yoga in schools?

- Was there such a thing as a children's yoga curriculum?

- What would happen if we engaged teachers by offering/using some basic aspects of yoga in the classrooms so that children could practice more yoga more often and so that the teacher could benefit also?

This line of questioning led me to consider seriously the idea of forming a nonprofit entity focused on teaching yoga to children in school settings and training their teachers. This meant that I would have to bring other children's yoga teachers on board.

The following year, Yoga in Schools (YIS) was born! Founding board members included two friends and my spouse, all attorneys, and me, as the Executive Director. I hired several intrepid yoga teachers who had experience working with kids to help with the initial teaching load. We received a grant from the Grable Foundation for $34,000 to conduct a 16-week pilot study in three inner-city schools: a public school, the charter school I had been serving, and a small independent Christian school. Life became full to overflowing. I was making a difference in children's lives and making a living employing others to do the same. What a dream!

Ten or so years removed from this bold, strong, surprising start, I am even more grateful to foundations like the Grable Foundation. They took a chance on us, and it paid off. We got our start in designing and delivering school-based programming, taught yoga to teachers and students, collected data, and did what we said we would do: (1) Provide teachers with classroom and self-help tools to manage emotional and physical stress; (2) Positively affect children's social and psychological development in terms of self-esteem (confidence, efficacy) and body awareness; (3) Positively affect children's academic development in terms of concentration and classroom behavior; and (4) Improve children's flexibility, balance, and relaxation skills.

In pursuit of these objectives, we learned many things. For instance, positively promoting children's self-esteem and body awareness can be done in an inclusive setting. Some children's bodies may not quite "fit" the standard for team sports or skill-based activities. YIS assistants, all yoga teachers trained in kids-yoga and who have experience working in schools, made a crucial difference in achieving 100% participation and benefit! Sometimes it was merely a look from an assistant teacher (AT)—or perhaps the AT placing herself beside the child struggling to focus—that allowed the class to continue without incident. There is a real art to being an AT without usurping the authority of the lead teacher and not creating a distraction by dealing with the differing needs of the students. Many times the lead teacher would not be aware of the "fires" being put out by the AT, allowing the lead teacher to continue leading and demonstrating without distraction—a vital focal component of a children's yoga class with urban youth.

The primary lesson we learned from this pilot study was the need to invest in the adults tied to YIS programming as carefully as investing in YIS curriculum mastery and classroom techniques. Teachers, school administrators, and YIS staff were key to the successful integration of school-based yoga programming. This is still true today.

After the pilot study, we were able to leverage the resulting goodwill and gain access to other foundations such as the Buhl Foundation, the Sampson Foundation and, eventually, the Heinz Endowments. The process seems similar to building one's credit rating.

Since its incorporation in 2005, YIS has worked with many school districts and operated in different ways. We have brought in children's yoga teachers to teach the children directly. We have taught school teachers, counselors, administrators (including superintendents), and behavior specialists to use basic yoga movements and simple breathing exercises at their desks and with their students. We have implemented one- and two-year professional development programs for Health & Physical Education (HPE) teachers so they would be equipped to teach yoga as part of HPE. Furthermore, we have developed a curriculum specific to the needs of busy HPE teachers and have implemented district-wide trainings.

An Alternative School Story

Recently, we have been working with the Rankin Promise Program (RPP), an alternative school in the small, urban, Woodland Hills School District in Pittsburgh, Pennsylvania.

We provided programming at RPP for four years, though the first two years were part of a district-wide staff training which included yoga as PE, yoga as teacher self-care, and yoga skills for the classroom. The students at RPP are 99% African American, and all of them receive free and reduced lunch. During that time, there have been four principals. However, the teaching staff has remained fairly stable. Beyond the first two years working with the district, our goals for RPP were (1) an increase in the regularity and frequency of classroom use of yoga tools, and (2) the inclusion of direct student education in social-emotional learning (SEL) and emotional health in addition to yoga movement and breathing exercises. Specifically, I taught three classes each week that included yoga movement, breath and mindfulness exercises, and SEL principles. I also provided staff training and curriculum resources and continued weekly visits to the school to offer professional, specialized counseling services that supported the well-being and self-care of students and staff alike.

Our success and progress have required several years of steady outreach and quiet, friendly interest in the staff as individual people who have lives beyond the walls of the school. Some people have pleasantly surprised me with their interest in yoga both in school and for themselves personally. I continue to represent quiet strength and calm. From my observations, I think every school needs a "wellness specialist/resource person" who walks the halls checking in with all staff and finding out how to be of service to them. With the passing of time, the RPP staff came to believe I was theirs—to be of service to them and the students.

My role shifted to be a resource to teachers and to use yoga as a therapeutic intervention with individual students who were part of the Mental Health Partnership (MHP) and its partner agency, Glade Run Lutheran Services. The application of yoga as therapy one-on-one is very potent. It was an exciting opportunity to work individually with students. In previous years, I have run therapeutic yoga groups with children in special education. This is extremely hard work, even with a small group. Deregulated children are difficult to manage. Some behaviors I have observed include the students' side conversations—when the children will be either chatty or argumentative with one another and not be able to hear my instructions. In addition, another child across the room may jump into a side conversation or make a comment, all of which causes more disruption. Gaining control of the class should happen before the children even enter the classroom. I find it to be very effective to meet my students at the door, call them by name, and let them know what we will be doing or find out what they would like to do. I like to include time to honor their requests, if possible, whether it is a particular pose or a game or song. This helps to give them "buy in" or ownership in the learning process.

It is a completely different story to work with some of these same children individually. They are often delightful, curious, polite, and genuinely interested in learning ways to address their challenging behaviors. Some have a good sense of awareness of what they need to work on, such as managing anger or staying on task. The students are quite receptive to yoga. The average length of stay for students at the RPP school is 45 days. During that time, I saw each child only 4 or 5 times if they are in attendance on the same day I was at the school. I am struck by just how much a simple yoga practice has to offer these kids. I nearly always included six movements of the spine with breathing, sun salutes, and a game called "Yogi Says." Of particular interest to the children was breathing with the Breathing Wheel (a small plastic Frisbee I purchased from an ad specialty company), which opens and closes and helps children immediately "get" how to use the breath to calm down.

I tried to let each session be led by the child's interests. I helped them identify something they would like to work on that day. Typically my toolkit includes chimes; a small, portable aromatherapy diffuser; a breathing wheel (as mentioned above); Move With Me Adventure Skill Cards; some fun, upbeat music (like Kira Willey's "Dance for the Sun" album); and some quiet soothing instrumental music coupled with an age-appropriate visualization.

I felt welcome and supported as a yoga instructor at RPP, but it took several years for the teachers, behavioral specialists, security officers, and aides to actually take my role seriously. The behavioral specialists and the teachers at Rankin are now yoga advocates and allies. I have overheard several teachers recommending/encouraging their students to come and see me. Not long ago, I was chatting to a behavioral specialist in the hallway, and he said he tried to explain to a student all the reasons that yoga would be helpful to him. This kind of support makes my job a lot easier. Right after the behavioral specialist had this conversation with this particular student, the student, who was agitated, actually stopped, faced me and heard me out for a few minutes. I then was able to acknowledge that he was already having a rough day, and he agreed to work with me the following week even though he did not want to have a session that day. This was a breakthrough both with the student and with the behavioral specialist who was supporting the student.

Classroom Management

Over the years, we have experienced many noteworthy incidents that have created "aha" moments. One that sticks in my mind occurred during one of our first teaching opportunities at Helen S. Faison Arts Academy in Homewood, arguably one of the toughest elementary schools in the Pittsburgh Public Schools system. On a day not too long into our 16-week pilot study, I was teaching a class of about 29 fifth graders.

The teacher next door was a friendly but no-nonsense teacher called Mr. Andrews, who also happened to be built like a linebacker. He had checked in with me several times and told me to call upon him if I needed help with anything. I was glad for the offer but not sure how I would summon him if I actually needed help. Presumably, he was thinking along the same lines, because he said, "just yell if you need me." Well, on this particular day, even though things had started well and we were heading into a nice round of sun salutes, I turned my back for a second to cue my music (big mistake) and heard a crash as a kid jumped on another kid and began fighting. I had not seen it coming (I now see how hard it is to keep one's eyes on 29 students), but I knew I had to act fast, or I would have a "dog pile" on my hands (where everyone jumps on the kid who is down).

I ran to the door and yelled for Mr. Andrews. He seemed like he knew I would call. He gave a quick directive to his classroom and was in my doorway immediately with a "what's going on?" bellow. I just pointed to the two offenders. His "linebacker" features came in handy as Mr. Andrews just picked up a kid in each one of his meaty paws and half-carried, half-walked them out. All of this action took but a minute or two—not a lot of time to regain my composure—but in that minute, I had a decision to make. I drew myself up as tall as possible and said, "That was unfortunate, but let's do our sun salutes," and off we went. Stunningly, the students all followed my lead.

Perhaps that story does not sound very dramatic, but, believe me, that result was highly unusual. For the kids not yet in the fight to refrain from jumping into the fray and, instead, to actually engage with me at that moment was a very big deal. These kids chose yoga over fighting. Concurrent with my Yoga In Schools efforts, I had been working with adults and teens as a psychiatric social worker in a venue where I had robust infrastructure to contain any safety issues very quickly. Classroom teachers do not have the same supports and have to rely largely on their verbal skills to diffuse escalating behaviors. Many teachers do not feel qualified to do this. While I empathize, I think that trouble-shooting and de-escalation are necessary skills to have as a teacher. Lucky for me as a newbie teacher, I had Mr. Andrews to "rescue" me. However, giving a clear directive and opportunity for all of us to "move on" after the incident was critical.

Later, I was able to acknowledge the students for their choices and remind them of what could have happened. I also debriefed with the two students who were removed from the classroom. They had a two-week break from yoga, which was the decision I made at the time, and they were invited to return afterward. Subsequent classes went more smoothly than before. Perhaps it was the right decision to remove them for a time, although I second-guessed many of my classroom management decisions, particularly in the early years. Now, as a veteran educator of students (adults and children) with mood disorders and emotional dysregulation, I have a bigger classroom management toolbox from which to draw. Moreover, my experience has helped me set clear boundaries sooner and use fun and engaging practices to draw the class together. I have also learned that thinking on my feet is important and that having a backup plan is essential. Whenever possible, that plan includes enlisting others who will be ready to help when needed. I often use an upbeat piece of music at the beginning of my classes to engender some unity and familiarity—a beginning ritual of sorts that signals "we have begun our yoga time together."

Yoga is an "Inside Job": Training HPE Teachers

Another major realization has been that HPE teachers make very good yoga teachers when given adequate time and training. The learning of yoga postures and yoga breathing exercises is not a big stretch (no pun intended) for PE teachers. Often, they are surprised by how much they like the practice and even more surprised that their students like it. Often, too, we have seen initial resistance from teachers stemming from situations such as a lack of communication from the school district about required professional development. This kind of glitch has led to reactions such as "I'm not teaching "fx$&#g" yoga" or "these kids won't do yoga."

Over time, we have seen that, when the HPE teachers actually experience yoga for themselves and connect with their bodies in a more kindly way than they had previously, teaching yoga is a very natural extension of the skills they already have. One story in particular comes to mind of two high school teachers from Brashear High School (in the Pittsburgh Public School District) who took a little bit of yoga training and ran with it. We had been focusing on training K-8 HPE teachers in this district. To my knowledge, these two high school HPE teachers attended just one day of our training early in that school year. They contacted me for some additional support, because they had started a yoga program at their school by themselves, utilizing the information from their one-day of professional development with YIS and using Yoga Pretzel Cards (Guber & Kalish, 2005) as "start-up" tools.

I was very happy and encouraged to hear this. We met and brainstormed about ways to support their ideas. A huge step forward occurred when they reclaimed and cleaned out an old storage room next to the school's pool and made it into a yoga studio in a building where space is always at a premium. They wanted yoga mats, so they raised money by selling bottled water to their students. YIS was able to supply them with yoga blocks, which are used to help modify poses, and eye pillows, which are used at the end of class to help evoke the relaxation response. They tried some different formats and decided that they would offer yoga to all

9th graders the following year. Then, in 10th and 11th grade, yoga would be offered as an elective. In order to prepare better, they both participated in a 5-day Yoga Ed High School Training course during the summer. That fall they implemented the Yoga Ed curriculum. Their model met with the approval of the district's curriculum coordinator. The following year, it was adopted as a district-wide model for HPE. Friends, it does not get much better than that! My goal has always been to "work myself out of a job." It is an ideal situation when yoga programming comes from the inside, e.g., someone already working in the system.

Another story about HPE teachers making good yoga teachers arose from a performance-based assessment that was the culmination of teachers' two years of training for the Woodland Hills School District. Each teacher had to teach for 30 consecutive minutes (while we videoed). If they opted out of this, then they had to present a yoga class in person to their peers on the last day of training. As a result of this video assessment, we have documented "proof" of their abilities. I would say that they could "hold-their-own" with any other trained children's yoga teacher. This process also revealed a level of creativity by the teachers regarding how to include yoga as part of Health and Physical Education. On the final day of training, we showed the teachers a summarized version of their video assessments, allowing everyone to see everyone else's assessments. This is a rare occurrence among HPE teachers. They truly were able to appreciate each other's skill sets and expertise. Watching this whole process unfold was a beautiful thing.

Finally, we also arranged for the School District Superintendent to attend the final day of training and present each HPE teacher with a certificate and a YIS t-shirt. This was a meaningful experience for all of us. The whole day involved HPE teachers leading their peers and YIS staff in yoga practices. I will never forget how happy and satisfied I felt that day, lying in resting pose in the gym being led in a beautiful visualization by an HPE teacher with all of his peers present and participating.

Act with Humility

Presenting yoga in schools has taught me many things. Near the top of the list is humility. Just when I thought that I had attained a level of mastery, I found out that I actually had not done so. For instance, on one occasion (maybe two), my class of 7 boys (at Rankin) had dropped to 3. When I inquired about the other four boys, I discovered that they had had a big fight in the hallway—on the way back to their classroom from yoga class with me! Now, before you comfort me or assure me that these things can happen, yes, I know they can, and my primary goal was to build skills with these boys while having fun doing yoga so they could self-regulate. However, what I know from my years of practicing and teaching yoga is that yoga also makes room for—and can promote or "stir up"—emotions that have been tamped down for a long time. Could the fight that had happened in the hallway have been caused by tamped down emotions erupting? The answer is "possibly." In knowing this, perhaps there was some added work/release/processing that could have been performed before sending the boys back to class. One of my roles as a qualitative researcher and observer is to notice (report) what things/facts/conditions change as a result of new learning. Our yoga session may have inadvertently "primed the pump" for a good old fistfight in the hallway. These painful observations are important things to be mindful of as we revise and tweak our programs.

Final Thoughts on Working with Schools

There are many things I want people to know about our work. For yoga teachers and service providers, I think it is important to build relationships with school stakeholders and figure out where your "in" is within the school district. This essential connection could come through parents, teachers, administrators, or even a school board member. Here are my recommendations: Start where there is an opportunity and interest. Then, do what you are asked to do or what you say you will do, and keep building from there—building relationships, building your program, building believers in your program. Even if your vision is big, keep your goals modest. Many educators want all new interventions to raise test scores. Don't promise that yoga will do this. Take your own medicine, and practice and model good self-care. Genuinely care for teachers and staff in the building. Read *Best Practices for Yoga in Schools* (Childress & Harper, 2015) to get a handle on what others who have come before you have done successfully.

When dealing with principals and school administrators, I often pitch ideas to them and take time to check in and see how they are doing and ask what they think their teachers need. Often the answers include things such as: provide a weekly staff yoga class; spend 5 to 10 minutes in each classroom once a week; help coordinate adjunct services in the building (like Glade Run Lutheran Services at RPP); help all staff understand each other's roles and how to best support one another so they have a sense that "someone has their back"; and identify individual teachers that may enjoy doing further yoga training and send them information. There are now many wonderful training programs to choose from—and several are represented in this book.

Beyond these practicalities, parents and teachers need to know that we want to continue giving children and teachers healthy body consciousness. This leads to a lifetime of functional movement patterns and an ability to regulate the breath to reduce stress and improve emotional well-being—something we all want for ourselves.

Andrea's Coda

Joanne is a close friend of mine. I worked as a consultant for Yoga in Schools and participated in planning and evaluating the district trainings that she mentions. I was the primary investigator on a case study of the alternative school where she provided direct instruction to students and support for staff. In the course of our work relationship, I have pushed Joanne to view schooling through the eyes of a teacher, as she has pushed me to see schooling from the point of view of a parent, adult educator, and a mental health professional. I continually bring in a structural analysis of schooling policies and staff behaviors, as she shows me how one person can take compassionate action in heavily constrained situations.

Joanne does not identify herself as White, and she is far more aware of being a woman in negotiating the implementation of her plans and in completing her programing goals. I have witnessed the way that men and boys treat her—a mixed bag of respect and patronization, though more of the former. Joanne is experienced with steadiness, fierceness in high-male power environments where I would not be so strong. Joanne grew up in Australia and her accent marks her as a "foreigner," no matter how many decades she has lived in the United States. She has always sought to capitalize on her own novelty rather than take offense at what others might perceive as mocking. Her educated Australian-accented English carries the privilege of being perceived as smart and interesting, rather than ignorant.

Joanne is aware of the over-representation of Black children in remedial education and the pathologizing of their behaviors (Dudley-Marling & Lucas, 2009; Losen & Orefield, 2002). Yet, she is not focused on calling out the educational mistreatment of traditionally marginalized populations, as I am, as a social justice educator and scholar. She lives in a majority Black neighborhood and she knows the people who live there as individuals, neighbors, friends, clients, and volunteer committee members. Joanne lives her Christianity as "her brothers' keeper," an international and domestic ambassador for peace and healing. She does not mention all of the volunteer work that she and her family do year-round. Her paid work with children is just a small part of what she does. In this way, she is like many of the women who write these chapters. They border on the harmfully selfless. What keeps them stable and replenished? They would probably say their families or their faith. I would guess, yoga.

Toward the end of her narrative, Joanne identifies herself as a qualitative researcher! I have encouraged her to see herself as a knowledge producer through co-authoring formal publications with her and helping her work through her first book outline. She did so much of the data collection and first-level analysis on our case study, I wonder that she did not say more about herself as a researcher. At the time of this writing, she is engaged in graduate study at the Pittsburgh Theological Seminary. I anticipate that her scholar-identity is getting stronger. I started this book project so that Joanne and the others could step into their roles as knowledge producers in the field of yoga in schools. Feminist research has long sought to elevate women's experiences and knowledge (for example, Belenky et al., 1997). Qualitative research is empowering to both researchers and their participants as it allows for human knowledge to emerge, though it lies outside of the discrete gaze of traditional, scientific research—parameters of the question being asked or the variable being tested.

References

Belenky, M. F., Clincher, B. M., Goldberger, N. R., & Tarule, J. M. (1997). *Women's ways of knowing: The development of self, voice and mind.* (Tenth anniversary edition). New York: Basic Books.

Childress, T., & Cohen-Harper, J. (Eds.). (2015). *Best practices for yoga in schools*. Atlanta, GA: Yoga Service Council/Omega Publications.

Dudley-Marling, C., & Lucas, K. (2009). Pathologizing the language and culture of poor children. *Language Arts, 86*(5), 362–370.

Guber, T., & Kalish, L. (2005). *Yoga Pretzels: 50 Fun Yoga Activities for Kids & Grownups*. Cambridge, MA: Barefoot Books.

Losen, D. J., & Orfield, G. (2002). *Racial inequity in special education*. Cambridge, MA: Harvard Education Publishing Group.

11

Practicing Yoga, Practicing Justice

PEG OLIVEIRA

"Do less, man. Do less."

—9th Grade Student

At New Haven Academy High School, the freshman class of 2017 arrived at school, fresh haircuts and skinny jeans, to be told that they would all be participating in mandatory yoga. Three times per week, for one hour and fifteen minutes each session, they would meet in the basement gymnasium, remove their shoes, and breathe their way to bliss. And, as could be expected, they were reasonably miffed. No gym this year. No basketball. Instead, warriors and down dogs.

During that first semester at NHA, I was guiding a class of 20 kids into savasana, having completed a practice with the message of simplicity: do less of the fidgeting and defending that causes friction and gets in the way of flow and authenticity. A usual suspect was tapping his fingers on the floor. First a minor rat-a-tat-tat. Then it gained a rhythm. Was it "Wrecking Ball"? "Get Lucky"? "Harlem Shake"! The tapping grew incessant.

My mind spun, considering how to encourage this student to come to stillness. I saw an English teacher, having joined us for yoga as many often did, sit up, also considering whether to say or do something to help the student pull it together. We locked eyes; hers rolled.

There entered the barely audible, just deep enough to be going on 15, voice of the football player body beside our fidgeting friend, say calmly, "Do less, man. Do less."

Life is Loud

Schools are loud. Trauma is loud. Life is loud. We talked a lot about noise; the kind you can't control outside your head like a neighbor's tapping fingers. And the kind you can control inside your head, like your reaction to the tapping. We practiced accompanied by a symphony of yelling teens, shouting teachers, rolling trash cans, clanging metal grates, and the incessant parade of people passing across our sky, literally. Our classes were in a dungeon; a basement gymnasium. It is deep and cavernous, and at one end, there is a catwalk. A perforated, metal bridge that connects one end of the school to the other through our firmament. Multiple times each day the janitor would wheel trash cans across sending a rhythmic metallic clunking through our space. Students would meander by and try to strike up a conversation from above. Liability concerns kept us from being allowed to board up the walls of the bridge. But leadership acquiesced to a curtain. The result: cloaked in anonymity, ghost silhouettes running past yelling "yoga" or "down dog."

I founded 108 Monkeys, a nonprofit yoga service organization, on the belief, as Martin Luther King Jr. said, that "true peace is not merely the absence of tension; it is the presence of justice." Service yoga is, for me, the marriage of my many passions and purposes as yoga teacher, social scientist, activist, and advocate for those whose voice has no microphone.

I finished my PhD in Psychology at age 30, and rather than seeking a professorship, as had been the master plan, I moved to New Haven, Connecticut, to work with a rock star nonprofit child advocacy organization. I geeked out on how to improve the child-care subsidy program to allow low-income families to access high-quality preschool. I marched for fair wages for early childhood educators. Before I was practicing yoga I was practicing justice.

But practicing yoga is also practicing justice. During those early years as an advocate, yoga found me. In a closet built lovingly by first-generation immigrants, over 10 years of Catholic school, eroding slowly from an undiagnosed pituitary tumor, yoga reminded me that justice starts at home. Through the trauma of illness, I forgot to maintain the me I had carefully built. Through yoga I remembered to be the me I was, but had forgotten. Truth emerged. And that truth was loud and, one heard, would not be unheard. Yoga echoed the teachings of justice I'd been taught back at St. Christopher's: to render to everyone what they deserve; including to myself. Yoga found me. It, and its inconvenient truths came, and stayed.

Osmosis is Not an Option

I was far from surprised that our newbie yogis lacked enthusiasm. I knew nothing, but I knew this; teaching yoga to 15 year olds in New Haven is no "if you build it they will come" proposition. Impact requires enticing sufficient participation in a student to release the neuro-restorative potentiality of yoga. They can't win if they don't play.

Others, however, were thrown. After all, who doesn't love yoga? One assistant yoga teacher joined our staff in September. Before the leaves fell from the trees he was gone. The students, he lectured me, were lazy, disrespectful, and didn't honor the great gift of yoga being offered and the sacrifices made to be there. Ski season was approaching! I agreed that the slopes would be a more gracious host, and bid him a tear-free good-bye.

Yoga with my students in poor, urban schools is not about teaching asana or making yoga more accessible. It's also not about building resilience, enduring, or staying the course. It is about raising consciousness. It is about acknowledging and accepting what is, as well as our individual and unique roles and responsibilities in that reality, and then, importantly, questioning the justice of the status quo and having the courage to propose a new path. Yoga practice is evolution. Yoga service is revolution.

Yoga offers only a few blunt tools—a mat, the breath, and the body. That's all I had to work with. I went in, scaffolding those tools with an arsenal of "feel your body" and "you must feel in order to heal" and "how does it feel to relax your belly?"

That was a bust. A decade of prior yoga teaching experience had in no way prepared me for the insistence of a 15 year old's "no." Will you . . . "no." Could you try . . . "no." Do you think you can . . . "um . . . no." These kids brought it. In every way. Not just in their resistance, but in their inquisition. Why? Why should I try that? Why would I ever want to do that? I had no good answers. I had answers, but they were not relevant. Because it feels good? Because you'll feel more energetic? Because you'll feel calmer?

They weren't drinking the Kool-Aid. And they were right not to. Yoga is a science of transformation. And change is hard. Evolution, by definition, requires letting go of what is in order to receive what could be. Some of us concluded, "It's like they like being tired and depressed!" That was shortsighted. It's not that our students didn't want to feel better or more energetic or calmer. It's just they had no data to believe yoga would do any of that. Yoga is an experiential practice. There is nothing to believe. You can't sell yoga; there's nothing to buy. It asks you to do and observe. I had to get them to do. Osmosis was not an option.

But I had already set myself up for failure. You want a teenager to dislike something, here's what you do. Make them do it.

Mandatory yoga. Imposed bliss. Required relaxation. Whose bright idea was this?

Mine.

While we had moderate success with elective yoga classes, I believed that if I could just get them to try it, yoga would work its magic and they would be as enticed by its trance as I was.

And just to make things more interesting, we set ourselves the goal of removing the usual sticks and carrots schools rely on. We informed everyone that as long as they attended and were respectful, they would pass. We never kicked anyone out of the yoga class for good, and on the few occasions that we did need to ask someone to step out for the remainder of that class, we made it clear that they returned for the next class with a clean slate. And we lived up to that promise. Even when it was hard.

Even when Jordan, all 6 feet and 2 inches of basketball superstar of him, pushed too hard one Friday afternoon. What started as a drip-drip-drip of opposition turned quickly to a constant stream of obscenities and distractions, resulting in a standoff. A standoff is where I never want to be. It means I've already lost. But that's where we landed; me outside the gym trying to coax the security guard to go inside and escort Jordan to the Dean's office, where he refused to go. And the security guard rambling through a litany of excuses why he shouldn't do his job. When we finally got Jordan out, as he passed me in the hall, glaring, I said, "You better have your head on straighter tomorrow on the court. I'm watching you!" And congratulated him, Monday morning, back in class, for a game well played.

Jordan came to me in my second year of teaching at this high school. In my first year, however, I suffered the fate of all new teachers: the kid that still keeps me up at night. Mike joined an elective yoga class, much to everyone's surprise. Before I even had the roster, the school's director had prefaced saying, "Now we can remove Mike if it doesn't work out. But he wants to try. But we're prepared to put him in drumming if needed." Mike was a "frequent flyer"; often in trouble. As charismatic as he was insecure. Within a week of school, having had to have numerous sit-downs with Mike and the director, he decided to drop the class. I breathed a heavy sigh of relief, and wished him well.

If only I knew then what I know now. Since that first year, I've seen so many "Mikes" and I've been able to coach them and comfort them and convince them. They've stayed and together, we've grown. Mike was ready for me, but I wasn't ready for Mike.

In our mandatory yoga class, I couldn't bribe them with grades or threaten with expulsion. I couldn't lead a horse to water; I had to take the water to them. Instead, I made it worth their time to try. I figured out how to meet individual students and their unique needs and interests. Jason, for example, fancied himself a hockey star and came to life at the idea of improving his core stability and balance. Dynasty was a singer with stage fright and figured out that intentional breathing calmed her nerves.

One of our most energetic and frenetic freshman males in our mandatory yoga class brought challenges ranging from napping to screaming racial and homophobic slurs at peers and teachers, to a climactic moment of physically assaulting a fellow yogi. Tempted as we were to ask him to leave, he begged to stay. I allowed it, but with a slate of requirements, including an amped up staff-to-child ratio. He made it through the semester, I finally stopped holding my breath, celebrated his success, and wished him a happy winter break. And when we returned in January, guess whose name was on the roster in our elective yoga class. I was incapable of holding back. "You are blowing my mind!" I told him. "Why, why, why are you back?"

"Miss, I like yoga."

Bodies Need

None of this is easy. Yoga isn't easy. In fact it's excruciating. Yoga asks us to remember the inconvenient truth that we have a body. For some of us, that's annoying, but surmountable. For others, not so much.

Bodies need.

They need food. They need sleep. They need attention; medical and more. They have desires and they don't take no for an answer. They are billboards of our every scar and tear. Like a broken record, bodies force us to replay memories we wish to forget. They won't forget.

Poverty only amplifies the inconvenience of the body. More than one in five American children are currently living in poverty; higher than ever before. There is growing evidence that financial insecurity increases someone's odds of poor psychological and physical well-being (Chetty, Stepner, & Abraham, 2016). When compared with all children, poor children are more likely to have poor health and chronic health conditions (Bradley & Corwyn, 2002). The opportunity to run around in open, safe, clean spaces with decent air quality is lacking in our urban districts (Calderon-Garciduenas et al., 2014). Everyone is tired. Many of our kids are hungry and malnourished. One high school teacher thoughtfully criticized our previous use of the term "yoga snacks" telling us that if we advertised a snack, we'd "better be packin' pizza."

And let's face it, school is no place for a body. Schools deal with brains, presupposing a needless body. Lunch might be at 11 a.m., ready or not. Please pee at the bell; not before or after. Unless you are a teacher, then don't pee at all. And sit without moving for six hours straight. No fresh air until 3 p.m.!

Are You Safe?

When I called roadside assistance for my flat tire, the attendant answered asking, "Are you safe?" Right! First, we need to be safe. Then we can deal with the crisis.

In a myopic imposition of my own experience, I started at "feel." But feeling is not Yoga 101. Feeling is not at the base of the pyramid. I'd been tripping over my own experience as a yoga teacher. I needed to step back, put on my "developmental psychologist" hat and go back to basics.

In spite of popular belief, kids have impeccable reasons for how they act. They are more reasonable than we give them credit for. Organically they knew they were not ready to feel. Are you safe? Are you connected? That's Yoga 101. Not until I created a safe and secure space for the soul could I engage the body. Not until I helped them experience strong attachments and connections would they take risks and try. This was fundamental to introducing feelings without confusing feelings with self. Without being overwhelmed in feeling. Without it feeling like feeling might kill us.

Trauma, by definition, is living in the past. It's being impacted now, in your own mind, by something that isn't happening now, outside of your own mind. It's the curse of being somewhere, not here, now. "Mindfulness is awareness that arises through paying attention, on purpose, in the present moment, non-judgmentally," says Jon Kabat-Zinn (https://www.mindful.org/jon-kabat-zinn-defining-mindfulness/). Practically speaking, trauma is the anti-mindfulness.

And it's the norm for most. In fact, 64% of our population has experienced at least one or more event in their first 18 years of life that qualifies them as having experienced trauma. In poor communities trauma is even more prevalent.

Don't Let Anybody Steal Your Peace

Yoga is union. It is relief to trauma's disconnection. Practicing yoga together, as a group, creates a laboratory for social connection and growth.

Our first few weeks (ok, months) of the fall saw lots of giving up, and comments about their own and each other's limitations. By winter break, we'd grown more supportive of each other's efforts, and more willing to help other students by offering them tips and encouragement; we were each other's cheerleaders. There was more optimism about their own abilities as well, and they were more likely to try new and challenging poses, like a headstand or an arm balance. Even the few students who did not participate much at the start of the semester began participating regularly. Some things were sticking.

One concept that seemed to immediately resonate was the idea that "peace of mind" is always available if they choose to actively focus, rather than reacting to whoever or whatever was distracting them. I saw bodies attend in agreement to "Don't let anybody steal your peace." Several students visibly took it to heart. They started practicing with their eyes closed. An exceptionally tall and talkative student who struggles with balance (both physical and emotional), decided to turn her mat toward the wall and away from her friends during balancing poses. In doing so, she did much more than improve her focus during tree pose—she demonstrated a grasp of the concept, by quietly taking action to help herself choose what to allow to take up space in her attention. Another student shared, "If you stay in your space and you really focus no one can mess that up. All you have to do is try."

One winter afternoon, during our closing circle, an orange Crayola marker swooped down on us from the overhead bridge, pegging Marco upside the head. Footsteps were heard clanking across the bridge and down the hall. Marco sprang, and ran out the door, but then suddenly casually returned and took his seat in the circle. I marveled out loud at his composure. I celebrated the "yoga off the mat" moment of not letting anyone steal our peace! I commended him for pulling it together, not even swearing. He said "I did swear, but not a bad swear." We agreed to call it a win, nonetheless.

And We Connect More

At the core of the doing body is a silence of being.

The body is the home of this innate silence. The body is silence, manifesting. It is the dance of Shiva around the silent still point of Shakti. It's not the imposed silence of power. It's not the silencing of authenticity. This is the organic silence that allows us to hear ourselves and hear the other and, in the quiet, our commonality. Silence is irreducible. It is elemental. Silence precedes justice.

I had thought teaching was about the wisdom of what I said. It's not. It's in the wisdom of knowing when to shut up. How to create a safe space in which to rest; to pause, reflect, and maybe then respond rather than react.

In our high-need urban schools, heavily infused with rules and boundaries and hierarchies, yoga is the great equalizer. It is not a therapy. It is not a class; it is a shared communal event. Students become leaders. Teachers become students. Students become teachers to teachers. Roles and boundaries fall away. A new set of often unspoken and democratic norms and ethics, rather than rules, organically evolve, and take hold. They belong to all and for all.

And in that gym-turned-studio sacred space, we learn to speak the same language. Silence. We know how it feels. We know what it means. And we earnestly and respectfully practice communicating with each other; in silence.

We do less. And connect more.

Janet's Coda

In this chapter, Peg complicates two common narratives regarding yoga in schools (and in this book): first, that "if you build it, they will come" and second, that the primary purpose of offering yoga in schools is to foster student resilience. Her respect for youth, acknowledgment of how schools position them in deficit ways, and commitment to social justice reveals some, as she puts it, "inconvenient truths" about yoga in schools.

By refusing to pathologize or blame students for their resistance, Peg listened to their questions and understood that they didn't believe the promises of yoga, i.e., it will make you calmer, more energetic, feel better. They had no evidence, which makes their resistance a pretty sound decision, even as it meant they would not have access to yoga's benefits. Making yoga available was not enough, so it became mandatory to ensure they participated. Within that schooling discourse of power, though, she inserted the yoga discourse that showing up is enough. All students had to do to pass the class was attend and be respectful. This blending of two disparate discourses provided incentive for students to do it ("I have to") without making it a win/lose situation. This sense of safety within familiar boundaries allowed them the opportunity to take the risk of engaging in yoga.

One of the key parts of this chapter is the acknowledgment of that risk, and that students must feel safe before being ready to feel what is happening in their bodies and minds. Many youth, especially in impoverished areas, have experienced trauma and may not be ready yet to engage in practices that ask them to look deeply into themselves and their experiences. Schools are not set up to approach students with the necessary tenderness. By teaching that peace is something they can choose through attentiveness, Peg offered them agency in dealing with their feelings.

For Peg, yoga's relationship with justice is not about teaching students to be resilient in the face of poverty and racism. Instead, by fostering inner peace through permission to be silent enough to listen to the body, to reflect and respond, and to share leadership in community, justice becomes an organic, democratic experience where everyone's value is acknowledged. This is not about fixing students or providing them with something they are missing; but rather offering a path that they may or may not be ready to take.

In an interview with Krista Tippett, the philosopher Jean Vanier said that we don't know what to do with our own pain, and yet we try to manage the pain of others. As yoga service providers, we may want to consider whether our role is to echo the educational system by teaching youth how to become capable citizens, which is prevalent in the language of resilience, social emotional learning, and the like. While that is certainly valuable, Vanier suggests that ". . . it's not quite the same thing as to educate people to relate, to listen, to help people become themselves" (Tippett, 2016, p. 84). This thorough attention to the student requires more than a yoga curriculum, no matter how well-crafted. It requires a willingness to really see the students and to take the time to let them tell us their stories in whatever form they choose.

That perspective, though, does not reconcile with the requirements of school, particularly when yoga service providers have worked so hard to make yoga acceptable by removing many of its holistic, spiritual aspects (Horton, 2016). What I find most provocative about Peg's chapter is to revisit the question of why we believe yoga in schools is important, and for whom? Are we offering the practices to support students or to ask them to reconcile with a system that has oppressed them?

References

Bradley, R. H., & Corwyn, R. F. (2002). Socioeconomic status and child development. *Annual Review of Psychology, 53*, 371–399.

Calderon-Garciduenas, L., Torres-Jardon, R., Kulesza, R., Park, S., & D'Angiulli, A. (2014). Air pollution and detrimental effects on children's brain. The need for a multidisciplinary approach to the issue complexity and challenges. *Frontiers in Human Neuroscience, 8*(613). DOI: 10.3389/fnhum.2014.00613.

Centers for Disease Control and Prevention, Kaiser Permanente. (2016). The ACE Study Survey Data [Unpublished Data]. Atlanta, GA: U.S. Department of Health and Human Services, Centers for Disease Control and Prevention.

Chetty, R., Stepner, M., & Abraham, S. (2016). The association between income and life expectancy in the United States, 2001–2014. New York: *Journal of the American Medical Association, 315*(16): 1750–1766. DOI: 10.1001/jama.2016.4226.

Horton, C. (2016). Yoga is not dodgeball: Mind-body integration and progressive education. In B. Berila, M. Klein, and C. Jackson Roberts (Eds.). *Yoga, the body and embodied social change* (109–124). Lanham, MD: Lexington Books.

Kabat-Zinn, J. Mindful: Taking time for what matters. Retrieved from https://www.mindful.org/jon-kabat-zinn-defining-mindfulness/.

Tippett, K. (2016). *Becoming wise: An inquiry into the mystery and art of living.* New York: Penguin.

Conclusion

A Place for Making Meaning

Andrea M. Hyde and Janet D. Johnson

In this final chapter, we ground yoga within a larger framework of social justice and responsibility, reinforcing our feminist framework. Beginning with full recognition of how the tensions in this book reflect the larger culture of yoga in the United States, and then yoga in schools, we analyze our learning as it has emerged from working with our contributors on their narratives. We reflect on the entire project: our goals, the process of working with each other, and the rightness or fit in using narrative inquiry for the book. We conclude with a summary statement based on the themes that arose from our contributors' chapters, called "This is What We Know about Yoga in Schools."

Privilege and Yoga: Race and Gender

This book amplifies yoga teachers' voices within the school yoga community and credits them with contributing to this field of knowledge. For historical and material reasons acknowledged throughout this text, that group is overwhelmingly made up of white, middle-class women, which reflects the demographics of U.S. yoga teachers and public educators in general. It also necessarily limits the scope of this research and, we would argue, the entire field of yoga research in schools. For middle-class and wealthy white women, yoga is a culturally sanctioned and economical feasible activity. Few yoga teachers make enough money to support themselves, let alone a family, so yoga teaching is often seen as a boutique endeavor or a voluntary service activity. For this reason, we applaud the work of yogis such as Beth Berila, Melanie Klein, and Chelsea Jackson Roberts (2016) who analyze why certain groups—people of color, members of the LGBTQ community, poor and working-class folks—are often excluded from yoga spaces.

The editors and contributors of this volume are both privileged and marginalized. Though some of us are boundary crossers (hooks, 2000) and identify with more complex social backgrounds and identities, we are white, middle-class, professional women. We occupy the intersection of these status categories, and/or we are perceived this way, and enjoy the privileges and suffer the limitations associated with these identifiers. Almost all have advanced academic credentials, though only we (Andrea and Janet) have academic rank as university faculty. In the field of research, we are still the minority but this is rapidly changing (Elsevier, 2017).

We want to recognize yogis who do not fit the traditional yoga teacher category, who by their very bodies and their experiences are welcoming Others to yoga. These are just of few of our colleagues in the school yoga community: Atman Smith, Ali Smith and Andres Gonzales of Holistic Life Foundation in Baltimore, Krishna Kaur Khalsa of Y.O.G.A. for Youth in Los Angeles, Chelsea Jackson Roberts of Red Clay Yoga in Atlanta, Michelle Mitchell of YoKid (and the National Kids Yoga Conference), Bidyut Bose of Niroga Institute in Oakland, and Felicia Savage of Yoga Roots on Location in Pittsburgh. We also deeply value the work of decolonizingyoga.com for providing a platform to discuss how yoga, as practiced in U.S. studios and portrayed in marketing, reinscribes a narrow image of who belongs in a yoga class. This site regularly posts articles and videos on how yogis are making their studios or teaching practices more inclusive, particularly by supporting classes specifically for students who are queer, full-bodied, disabled, or people of color.

Race, class, and gender, as noted in multiple places in this book, shape our lens of experience and the stories we tell. Many of our contributors were already confident in their roles as educators and had some authority as such. White people carry more of an expectation of success and less of an apprehension of difficulty (David, 2014) because of historical structures that have made these outcomes likely, and partly because whiteness (a purposeful construction) was originally given as a "compensatory wage" to poor white people (duBois, 1966/1935). Real or perceived middle-class status multiplies this privilege, which Iris Marion Young (2009) called "respectability" (p. 41). Because privilege is relative (McIntosh, 1988; Tatum, 2003; Utt, 2012), sexism reduces this and other aspects of white privilege for women, while classism amplifies it for affluent women. Our contributors' stories, then, are grounded in their lived experiences and perspectives as middle-class, white women. That said, their stories are not static or monolithic; instead they reflect the complexity of their geographic, professional, and social locations (Yoon, 2016). As Yoon notes, educators' stories can serve to perpetuate dominant narratives that position students as Other, or they can be transformative. We believe that our contributors' stories are in the latter category. Not only do they transform the field of yoga research, they provide insider perspectives on yoga in schools.

Ontologies and Epistemologies: Theories of Personal and Social Change

Throughout this book, we have attempted to name the divergences we see within the field of school yoga. In chapter 1, we outlined the epistemological and ontological differences between traditional scientific research and qualitative projects such as this one, while arguing that both kinds of research provide important understandings of the field. In chapter 2, we took a feminist-relational approach and described the tensions and limitations of this project, including the lack of teachers of color and difficulties in trying to reach multiple audiences, i.e., yoga teachers, school personnel, and yoga scholars. Here, we describe how some of our contributors' ontologies, or theories of existence, differ from ours, and how we worked to reconcile them.

We are both students and teachers of critical contemplative pedagogies (Berila, 2016; Kaufman, 2017) and are both engaged in reading and writing in this interdisciplinary field that joins anti-oppressive praxis with contemplative philosophy and practice. That is, we understand how power is inscribed on minds and bodies and believe that mindfulness and yoga can be personally and socially transformative, even as they can also reinscribe what counts as appropriate behavior or value as a physical body. Because of this critical theoretical orientation, our inclination was to look for how and when our contributors named these issues, but most of them did not. Instead, many of our contributors' stories were primarily oriented by what Schiro, a curriculum theorist, would call a "learner-centered" approach (2015), meaning that personal knowledge is valued and the needs and concerns of individuals are paramount. In developing their own theories of inequity based on their experiences, many of the contributors' solutions rested in the individual. For example, they often described their work in terms of helping students and teachers improve their overall health with some framing the purpose of this work as being better school outcomes. This echoes how yoga is usually taught across multiple contexts: yogis observe their emotions, minds, and bodies to stimulate awareness and cultivate control. As educational scholars, Andrea in social foundations and Janet in literacy, we are more critically oriented toward structural (social) analysis, or what Schiro names as "social-reconstructionist," and this is evident in our writing. While we value and use aspects of the learner-centered approach, we believe that changing inequitable systems requires teaching students to recognize how privilege shapes individual experience, and to offer explicit ways to engage in positive social change. Our contributors may agree, though these stories do not contain much structural criticism. We highlighted the authors' social and critical positions in the chapters' codas.

The tensions between learner-centered and social reconstructionist ideologies are familiar to us because most of our undergraduate and some of our graduate students adopt a primarily learner-centered view of educational phenomena. As teacher educators, we take seriously our role in teaching critical perspectives to current and future teachers, as we believe their work is crucial to systemic change. We expose students to critical thought and structural analysis, pushing their thinking by asking them to uncover the foundations of their taken-for-granted beliefs. As editors, however, we wanted the contributors to tell their stories with a minimum of interference from us. If we had urged them to be more explicitly critical, their stories might not have been as authentic. Taking the feminist relational "both/and" frame described in chapter 2 allowed us to balance and value both the learner-centered and social-reconstructionist approaches.

On a related note, we found ourselves wrestling with how much we value pragmatic, learner-centered work described by many of the contributors, alongside our observations that the school yoga movement has followed disturbing trends we have seen in multicultural education and literacy education. Gloria Ladson-Billings notes that multicultural discourses, in some cases, have been appropriated to reinforce dominant ideologies instead of opposing them (2003). This happens when the historical and social experiences of people of color are distorted to reinforce ideas of otherness. She calls for "critical" multicultural education that offers a pedagogy of liberation and changed consciousness. Similarly, literacy educators have embraced progressive pedagogies that provide texts featuring people of color, which adds to a canon mostly populated with white, male authors. However, without an accompanying critical approach, these texts can reinforce othering and racism instead of questioning how systems affect individuals' choices and lived experiences. Scholars call for teaching these texts—and traditional texts—through a critical lens, with attention to how power is shaped according to race, class, gender, sexuality, and ability. They argue that transformation will not happen without attention to how inequities are embedded in systems, not just individual behaviors.

Similar debates are taking place in the scholarship of yoga in schools. As Janet has written elsewhere (under review), self-regulation and social-emotional learning can be seen as part of a growth mindset, championed by Carol Dweck (2007). Similar to the principle of pulling oneself up by the bootstraps, Dweck argues that dedication and hard work can overcome anything, including systemic oppression. The growth mindset requires students who live in the worst conditions, through no fault of their own, to set aside their experiences when they walk into school and to be emotionally aware and stable, something that many adults would not be able to do (Thomas, 2016). Other scholars note that the growth mindset and focus on self-regulation or social-emotional learning could be seen as racist by requiring individuals of color to act more white, thereby policing their emotions in the interest of schools, which are sources of power and authority (Boler, 1999). In naming non-normative student behaviors as being out of control, yoga curricula focusing on self-regulation might be seen as ignoring, and therefore perpetuating, systemic oppression.

While we are wary of school-based programs meant to correct individual behavior or academic achievement, a common social philosophy of those in the contemplative fields is that individual transformation is the necessary precursor to social transformation. Yoga programs teach the skills for self-transformation toward a healthier, happier way of being which extends the capacity for just action. When yoga becomes a priority for schools and teachers, students are provided with time to turn attention inward, which rarely happens during the school day.

We believe—and our contributors demonstrate—that yoga needs to be taught skillfully and intentionally. When the tools of yoga, such as breathwork and mindful movement, are explicitly named as empowering, then yoga becomes a path to liberation. Campano wrote,

> The realities of the heart and body are inherent in the nature of our inquiries and the very material from which we theorize our practice and shape our political stance . . . Sometimes our resistance takes an overt political form and is aligned with larger activist movements. Other times, it is more subtle but is resistance nonetheless; for example, our efforts to expand time and open up opportunities for reflection, creativity and bonding with our students may radically interrupt the institutional drive for efficiency and standardization. (2007, p. 116)

Any actions taken to create a more humanizing environment are part of transformation toward justice. Resistance does not have to be overt and critical; much of the work the contributors in this book describe does "expand time and open up opportunities for reflection, creativity and bonding" and therefore may actually disrupt trends toward "efficiency and standardization."

Even as we are still concerned about how yoga practices are often positioned in schools, i.e., as ways to get students to behave a certain way or do better on standardized tests, the contributors' stories demonstrate how students and teachers take these practices with them out into the world in positive ways. Therefore, we believe in the potential of yoga to awaken students to critical consciousness even as we recognize school as a place where systemic oppression is institutionalized.

Compassion as Social Justice

Awareness of social justice among the participants varied, as did their use of justice language, but the theme of compassion and care was salient for all of them. As her school's counselor, Debra created a yoga program for staff and students' mental health. Lisa, Joanne, and Michelle suffered illness, injury, and loss that brought them to yoga as a healing practice. They came into the schools as interested parents and community yoga teachers hoping to teach children how to heal and develop resilience to life's suffering. As a health educator, Dee brought yoga into her local schools to address violence prevention and bullying. Peg's narrative directly positions yoga as social justice work, and she consciously occupied the world of yoga service as a provider. Lindsay's story highlighted her efforts to teach healing practices to English language learners, identifying new immigrants and refugees for special concern. Carla addressed the challenges faced in schools by students from poor and working-class backgrounds.

Collectively, our contributors' ethical positions may be understood as compassion. Compassion for self and others must come before justice work because compassion is required to see injustice. Simply put, compassion is mindful and kind awareness of the condition of others. Without compassion, we are endlessly self-absorbed in a kind of madness that sees the entire universe as existing around ourselves as a unitary being (Wallace, 2009). Compassion develops in close proximity to others who are suffering; it comes from an examination of our own suffering and recognition of unity with others in this common human experience.

Co-founder and president of the Courage of Care Coalition, Brooke Lavelle (2016) observes that "[o]ne of the biggest obstacles we face to addressing structural and systemic issues is our deep individualistic cultural conditioning" (para. 19). Lavelle's work focuses on the intersection of contemplative practices and social justice, so she shares our concern that SEL programs can reinforce inequities by inadvertently reinforcing beliefs about historically marginalized populations as being in greater need of self-control. Framing ourselves as autonomous, independent selves "has limited our ability to see the complex ways in which our well-being is dependently linked to others and the institutions and structures within which we are embedded" (Lavelle, 2016, para 19). This is why we must push beyond a learner-centered philosophy of change, even as we recognize its value.

Fortunately, yoga and mindfulness programs have the potential to help people develop compassion through practices such as lovingkindness (Chodron, 1996), or heartfulness (Sofer, 2016). Lavelle suggests that they should also include overt lessons on ethical caring—being mutually interdependent with others by alternately taking on the roles of "the one caring" and "the one cared for" (Noddings, 1984). Lessons might then proceed through personal reflection to awaken recognition of systemic privilege in ways that are least likely to cause debilitating shame or denial (Hyde, 2013). At the same time, contemplative practices can help develop a positive, agentive identity for those who have been harmed by internalized oppression by growing up in a racist, (hetero) sexist, ableist, classist society (Berila, 2016).

Vulnerabilities

We see the willingness to be vulnerable as a key component of compassion and a trait that can be developed through yoga and mindfulness. For example, Lisa showed vulnerability by disclosing her depression and anorexia in the first sentence of her chapter, and Michelle wrote about her mother's suicide and her own struggles with depression. Other writers were reluctant to develop their proposed and accepted chapter into a first draft. They worried about the quality of their writing in consideration of what we (professors) must be used to, which we found amusing.

This vulnerability showed up not just in sharing deeply personal experiences, but for some, in finding a balance between storytelling and selling their programs. Brene Brown (2012) writes that U.S. norms of femininity include "showing modesty by not calling attention to one's talents or abilities" (p. 89). In working to mitigate some of the advertising or sales-speak in some chapters, contributors and editors acknowledged a shared distaste for ad language, a writing style that several of us developed to advance our service or educational programs. At the same time, we, the editors, reminded ourselves how women have historically had to battle with a double standard in self-promotion. Men who self-promote are seen as powerful, whereas it is seen as unseemly or inappropriate when women do it.

Even though sales language remains in some of the narratives, the overall message is how the authors came to occupy positions of respect and authority in the field of school yoga, and what they learned along the way. Women who call attention to their accomplishments have been socialized to internalize shame. Yoga and mindfulness support resilience in the face of shaming, and we acknowledge the contributors' successes as ways to claim their authority in this field.

Narrative as Telling and Knowing

In order to better understand the complexities and subtleties of yoga in schools noted above, we chose to base this book on narratives written by school yoga experts. Narrative inquiry provides a framework for studying how participants understand a particular phenomenon, in this case, their experience with yoga in schools (Bhattacharya, 2017). Narratives provide a specific kind of insider knowledge that demonstrates the narrator/author's unique perspective. While this is one of the limitations of narrative as empirical data, we believe it is important for researchers to understand the authors' subjectivities. In the codas, we analyze these data, just as we would any form of qualitative data.

Claiming Stories as Knowledge

Throughout this book, we argue that practitioner stories are invaluable in understanding what actually happens when yoga is introduced into public schools. As qualitative researchers using narrative methods, we are in the minority, and we know that some scientists would not call this work research at all. Randomized controlled trials are the gold standard for research in education as is the case with the natural and health sciences. The assumption here is that a controlled study design will most reliably measure an intervention's true effect (IES-NCEE, 2003). Understanding people's experiences is key to a deep analysis of the processes, effectiveness, and outcomes of phenomena, in this case, yoga programs.

Although relational methods may be used by either women or men, they are stigmatized as unreliable in some academic circles. They are, as Belenky et al. (1997) explain, women's ways of knowing. This is not an essentialist view of gender; rather, women were historically relegated to the private sphere and made responsible for the care of others. From marginalized positions, women developed what may or may not be their natural skills in language use and social organizing which led to persuasive political writing (Mary Wollstonecraft) and social work (Jane Adams) in addition to active subversion (Harriet Tubman) and economic action (Dolores Huerta).

Teachers, in general, should be recognized as knowledge producers and not just curriculum implementers and, lately, data trackers. The lower status of teachers-as-knowers is similarly related to teaching being associated with women. Horace Mann, the father of "common schools," argued for the replacement of Boston Masters with women because of their kinder dispositions and natural affinity for children (Tozer, Senese & Violas, 2013). Women as teachers fought for labor protections for themselves along with educational rights for Native Americans and emancipated slaves through the National Education Association (Holcomb, 2006). Still we have met many teachers who have internalized the idea of their work being vocational while, at the same time, defending their rights to be seen as professionals—remunerated, autonomous authorities. When an individual loves what she does, she will volunteer countless hours and advocate for the work in a selfless way. This work can be fulfilling. The problem is that our society tells women that they are expected to sacrifice for others, especially for children, thus complicating the choice of teaching as a profession for women. As two childfree women, we are keenly aware of this norm even in 2018.

The limitation in academia of what counts as published empirical research continues to confine the scope of "what we know" about school yoga to the narrow realm of only formal studies that have been published in science-oriented academic journals. While we are very much encouraged that our heretofore committed traditionalist colleagues are taking up qualitative methods and even qualitative designs, collections such as this one are necessary vehicles for recognizing and supporting the knowledge as narrative that does not qualify for these venues.

Contradiction and Collaboration

Stories are not told in a straight line. Stories are alive; rhizomatic. They are messy. This is why stories are suspect as evidence in trying to answer research questions or evaluate programs. The stories that the contributors tell in this volume—as well as the editors!—would change if told in another context, for a different purpose, or for a different audience. We found this same messiness in our collaboration, as we approached our authoring and editing based on our distinctive understandings of our roles as editors, our disciplinary perspectives, and even the diverse ways that we use the term narrative, which we outline below.

Because she sees stories as constructions from the beginning, Janet provided feedback to the authors with an eye toward improving readability for the wide audience of this book. She made suggestions for flow, adding dialogue and sections, and cutting repetition. She asked herself and the writer what sections and sentences were serving the theme or purpose of the piece, particularly in the context of this book. She saw this as different from teaching writing skills and practices, where the focus is on student learning, which may or may not lead to a "best" draft. Similar to her role as a writing teacher, though, she occasionally struggled with the line between supporting the author to make the best piece it could be versus maintaining the integrity of the author's original intent.

Andrea took a different approach to her role as editor, tending to think of the contributors' narratives as qualitative data that should be minimally altered. It was always a struggle for her to think of readability in traditional terms, though she recognized that this was necessary to the project as planned. Some of the contributors wrote in a circular manner; coming back over and over again to fill in details from previous parts of the story, jumping ahead to connect past to future with commentary from the present. For the sake of readability, Andrea asked that contributors adhere to a certain chronology, though she resisted shaping the narratives as much as Janet. To make our target word counts for each chapter, both Andrea and Janet had to cut some of the details of the stories; at times, Andrea felt like this was cutting the contributors' voices.

We spent enjoyable conversations expressing our differing views and implicit rules of editing the contributors' narratives and worked productively (and sometimes adversarially) through interpreting and representing our understandings of just what we had been doing throughout this project. When we finally focused on mining the contributors' stories as data for the inquiry project, *What do we know about yoga in schools?*, we remembered that researchers are always in the process of shaping data, no matter what paradigm or perspective they are taking. Parker and Zajonc write, "Phenomena are co-created by the observer and the world" (2010, p. 81), and we wanted to expose and explore this co-creation. Rarely do the authors of research projects disclose as much of the backstage goings on as we have; the concluding voice of the author is often definitive and unified, especially in traditional scientific research. As qualitative researchers *and* editors for this project, we have attempted to make our distinct subjectivities transparent throughout the book.

What We Know about Yoga in Schools

In this section, we describe what this project teaches us about school yoga that randomized control trials and other positivist research models cannot. We summarize the key learnings from this project as a combination of the emergent themes mined from the contributors' narratives and our reflection and extension of these themes in the codas. This summary is the fruit of the entire collaboration, demonstrating that even as narratives complicate what we think we know about a specific phenomenon (in this case, yoga in schools) it also provides a depth of knowledge unavailable from other forms of research. This project adds to the limited number of qualitative research studies as outlined in chapter 1.

From our analysis of the narratives in this collection, we argue that yoga in schools is about positive change that is personal, local, and undeniably social. We explicate this meta-theme below, loosely grouped in sections focused on students, adults, and programs.

Students

- School yoga addresses social inequities by teaching about the universal human experiences of challenge and ease. Most of the programs described in this collection focus on supporting students who are disadvantaged by the dominant culture or mainstream schooling. As school community members practice yoga together, they identify with each other as common fellows and wish each other well, which translates into less hostility and more harmony. Though many contributors recognized that school can be harsh for some children, when speaking of teaching yoga to students, joy and compassion are themes that emerged across almost all of the narratives. Yoga in schools, done well, teaches inclusiveness residually if not directly.

- Yoga offers children options for how to learn something about themselves and how to choose their mental and physical states. This is empowering, especially for a perpetually marginalized group who often have little control over their lives, particularly in school. Some contributors noted that yoga programs conflict with "best practices" behavioral management systems that operate on a reward and punishment system. Several narratives celebrated the opportunity to learn from students. School yoga programs often include opportunities for students to notice their inner states and develop the language to express their subjective experiences.

- Teaching yoga in schools is never separate from the emotional, social, economic, gendered, culturally specific environment of the school community. Effective school yoga programs directly address the tensions and emphasize the relationships within the school/community. Yoga teachers cannot ask students or other educators to put aside their situated realities, and yoga in schools rarely looks like what one might find in yoga studios, let alone what is shown in yoga magazines and on social media. Students practice yoga on their own terms and participate in determining which benefits of yoga are possible or desirable. Some students resist the practice or the teacher for one reason or another. That often means that progress looks very different than what someone may think it should. Sometimes participation is sitting quietly in the room; refraining from aggressing; showing up to class; allowing others to practice undisturbed; or being supportive of classmates who choose to engage in yoga.

- Yoga can benefit youth from a variety of social and demographic backgrounds. While most of the people who take yoga classes in studios in the U.S. are white, middle-class, able-bodied, straight cisgendered women (Berila, 2016), many school-based programs aim to specifically serve low-income and working-class, (political) minority background students. However, youth from more advantaged backgrounds benefit, too, as stress affects all and peace helps all. As the editors, we are vigilant about yoga being used as a way to stigmatize poor students perceived as having particular needs for self-control. At the same time we recognize, as do the contributors, that some youth live in more adverse situations than others. The stories here support the possibility that those with the most challenges to overall wellness reap the greatest benefits of yoga.

Teachers

- School-based yoga works best when taught to and practiced by adults first, and not in a merely instrumental way, i.e., to get kids to do it or so that teachers will be more skilled at instructing children in the practice. Instead, it must be intentional and thoughtful. Adults who work in schools are needful and deserving of yoga as much as the children. They are often transformed by the practice and their work with students is transformed as well. They become more resilient, yes, but also more happy and more fulfilled. When schools increase demands on teachers without the requisite time and support to accomplish their tasks, this creates a systemic barrier to teacher wellness and efficacy. Yoga programs that plan for teacher self-practice emphasize the importance of slowing down and doing less, encouraging teachers to reclaim time for themselves. This alone is a radical move toward a more humanizing school environment and has been recognized by scholars as important in higher education as well (Berg and Seeber, 2016).

- School yoga is facilitated by fully human, flawed and experienced yoga teachers who are familiar with life in schools, and who know something about child development and human relationships. Their personally transformative experiences moving from some level of suffering to living with more ease called them to share yoga with others.

Features of Quality Programs

- Effective programs need considerable thought for context-customized design, implementation, review, adjustment, and evaluation. These programs are logically and experientially derived, ethically grounded, technically sound, and always modified in their implementation. No one program will work for all individuals or groups; that is, there is no good way to "scale up" any one successful program or to replicate the experiences of one unique school community. Fidelity of implementation becomes less of a concern to teachers and researchers who understand this. Rich descriptions of yoga programs allow us to understand that variation is not a weakness or an indicator of program failure, but an indication of the community's unique needs.

- School yoga works best as a system-wide program that is supported by the top school administrators, the parents, the teachers, the staff, and the students. This can only happen when all have a chance to experience the program and comment on its design, organization, and evaluation. Many of the contributors recount their efforts on multiple fronts to facilitate that saturation of yoga into the entire school community, respecting their own limitations and working within the boundaries that are typical of bureaucratic institutions.

- School yoga is most effective when woven into physical, academic, social-emotional, and behavioral health curriculums. From physical education and health classes to before- and after-schools programs, and from classroom management to literacy and social-emotional learning, school yoga is infused throughout the day. More and more often, the distinction between yoga service provider and educator are blurred. Classroom teachers, special education teachers, social workers and counselors are natural allies to school yoga programs if not the yoga teachers themselves. Several contributors described their plans for developing internal capacity in schools to manage yoga programs with only minimal external support.

- Yoga in schools incorporates mindfulness and is sometimes called mindfulness or mindful movement or some other name besides yoga. Mindfulness means paying kind attention, on purpose, to the present moment. Mindfulness and yoga share the same purpose, to relieve suffering, by the same means, focused attention. However, yoga usually implies some kind of movement. The contributors differed in what they called their yoga programs for various reasons. Sometimes school yoga and mindfulness programs are treated as separate endeavors. The term mindfulness may command more attention because of its direct association in the United States with cognitive neuroscience, which enjoys authority and prestige in education research. Whatever the program or lessons may be called, the body, mind, and breath are yoked with present awareness and a foundation of self-compassion and equanimity.

- Yoga can facilitate teaching to the curriculum standards and learning goals that teachers are mandated to address in their teaching and assessments of students. As our contributors have noted, yoga pairs easily with social-emotional learning standards and health and physical education standards. It also works well for language learners in that it lowers their affective filter, presents socially enriching and pleasant activities that can be enjoyed without language competency, and empowers them to feel good in their bodies as vehicles for expression. Yoga provides students with sensory integration problems and social anxiety, such as those in autistic support classrooms, with low-stakes opportunities for reducing stimulation to a manageable and enjoyable level.

A Final Reflection

As the stories in this book demonstrate, yoga offers opportunities for teachers and students to engage in emotional and physical self-awareness and compassion, which can lead to more agentive identities. Meanwhile, qualitative research has the potential to humanize the entire enterprise of schooling. We believe that qualitative research on yoga in schools, written in accessible format by experienced practitioners and grounded in quality methods, widens and deepens the personal and public knowledge about this relational and primarily subjective phenomenon, and the teachers and students who are creating it daily. Writing and reading descriptive, first-hand accounts of school yoga programs and stories of yoga teaching could be the most valuable format for learning about what is happening in the yoga-in-schools movement holistically. Narratives such as the stories in this book follow the spirit of teacher action research, understood as a local, formative, personal and praxis-oriented inquiry undertaken by teachers for the purposes of learning and well-being for all involved (Gorski, 2017).

In this book, we highlight some of the potential and actual benefits of what school-based yoga may offer, while at the same time recognizing individual and systemic limitations to its widespread implementation. Schools are immersed in the current reign of data-driven decisions and social efficiency, which limit the full expression of any child's or teacher's interests and abilities, exacerbating already problematic opportunity gaps for non-mainstream youth and hindering the well-being of all. Yoga is not a magic bullet that will ameliorate the effects of material deprivation or the trauma of racism. No matter how self-aware or compassionate a child is, she is still part of systems that may not fully recognize or value what she brings to the world, depending on her multiple status category positions (race, class, gender, ability, language, etc.). We now call on others who have experienced yoga in schools to publicly share their stories, and for all of us to continue to develop what we know about yoga in schools, with awareness of the possibilities and constraints of schools impacted by neoliberal economic and social policies.

References

Arnove, R., & Torres, C. (2007). *Comparative education: Dialectic of the global and the local.* Lanham, MD: Rowman & Littlefield.

Belenky, M. F., Clinchy, B. M., Goldberger, N. R., & Tarule, J. M. (1997). *Women's ways of knowing: The development of self, voice, and mind* (10th anniversary edition). New York: Basic Books.

Berg, M., & Seeber, Barbara K. (2016). *The slow professor: Challenging the culture of speed in the Academy.* Toronto: University of Toronto Press.

Berila, B. (2016). *Integrating mindfulness into anti-oppression pedagogy: Social justice in higher education.* New York: Routledge.

Berila, B., Klein, M., & Jackson Roberts, C. (2016). *Yoga, the body, and embodied change: An intersectional feminist analysis.* Lanham, MD: Lexington Books.

Bhattacharya, K. (2017). *Fundamentals of qualitative research: A practical guide.* New York: Routledge.

Boler, M. (1999). *Feeling power: Emotions and education.* New York: Routledge.

Brown, B. (2012). *Daring greatly: How the courage to be vulnerable transforms the way we live, love, parent and lead.* New York: Gotham Books.

Butzer, B., LoRusso, A. M., Windsor, R., Riley, F., Frame, K., Khalsa, S. B., & Conboy, L. (2017): A qualitative examination of yoga for middle school adolescents. *Advances in School Mental Health Promotion.* DOI: 10.1080/1754730X.2017.1325328.

Campano, G. (2007). *Immigrant students and literacy: Reading, writing, and remembering.* New York: Teachers College Press.

Chodron, P. (1997). *When things fall apart: Heart advice for difficult times.* Boulder, CO: Shambhala Publications.

David, E. J. R. (Ed.). (2014). *Internalized oppression: The psychology of marginalized groups.* New York: Springer Publishing Co.

Du Bois, W. E. B. (1966/1935). *Black reconstruction in America: An essay toward a history of the part which black folk played in the attempt to reconstruct democracy in America, 1860–1880.* New York: Russell & Russell.

Dweck, C. (2007). *Mindset: The new psychology of success.* New York: Ballantine.

Elsevier. (2017). *Gender in the global research landscape.* Available at elsevier.com/research-intelligence/resource-library/gender-report.

Gorski, P. (2017). Teacher action research [Online]. Retrieved from http://www.edchange.org/multicultural/tar.html.

Holcomb, S. (2006). Answering the Call: A History of the National Education Association. *NEAToday* [Online]. Retrieved from http://www.nea.org/home/1704.htm.

hooks, b. (2000). *Where we stand: Class matters.* New York: Routledge.

Howe, K. R. (1998). The interpretive turn and the new debate in education. *Educational Researcher, 27*(8), 13–20.

Hoy, D. C. (2004). *Critical resistance: From poststructuralism to post-critique.* Cambridge, MA: MIT Press.

Hyde, A. (2013). The yoga of critical discourse. *Journal of Transformative Education, 11*(2):114–126. Retrieved from http://jtd.sagepub.com/content/11/2/114.full.pdf.

IES-NCEE. (2003). *Identifying and implementing educational practices supported by rigorous evidence: A user friendly guide.* Institute of Education Sciences, National Center for Educational Evaluation and Regional Assistance. Available at https://ies.ed.gov/ncee/pubs/evidence_based/evidence_based.asp.

Kaufman, P. (2017). Critical contemplative pedagogy. *Radical Pedagogy, 14*(1). Available from http://www.radicalpedagogy.org/radicalpedagogy.org/Kaufman.html.

Ladson-Billings, G. (2003). *Critical race theory perspectives on the social studies: The profession, policies, and curriculum.* New York: Information Age Publishing.

Lavelle, B. (2016, November 16). A call for more compassionate, equitable education [Web post]. Retrieved from http://courageofcare.org/uncategorized/a-call-for-more-compassionate-equitable-education/.

McIntosh, P. (1988). *White privilege and male privilege: A personal account of coming to see correspondences through work in women's studies.* Wellesley MA: Wellesley College Center for Research on Women. Retrieved from http://www.worldcat.org/title/white-privilege-and-male-privilege-a-personal-account-of-coming-to-see-correspondences-through-work-in-womens-studies/oclc/19756670.

Noblit, G. W. (2004). Reinscribing critique in educational ethnography: Critical and postcritical ethnography. In K. de Marrais & S. Lapan (Ed.), *Foundations for research: Methods of inquiry in education and the social sciences* (pp. 181–202). Mahwah, NJ: Lawrence Erlbaum and Associates.

Noddings, N. (1984). *Caring: A feminine approach to ethics and moral education.* Berkeley: University of California Press.

Palmer, P. J., Zajonc, A., & Scribner, M. (2010). *The heart of higher education: A call to renewal.* San Francisco, CA: Jossey-Bass.

Peters, M., Burbules, N. (2004). *Poststructuralism and educational research.* Lanham, MD: Rowman & Littlefield.

Schiro, M. (2015). *Curriculum theory: Conflicting theories and enduring concerns.* Los Angeles: Sage.

Sofer, O. (2016, April 8). Heartfulness practice [Web post]. Retrieved from http://www.mindfulschools.org/personal-practice/heartfulness-practice/.

Tatum, B. D. (2003). *Why are all the black kids sitting together in the cafeteria? And other conversations about race* (2nd ed.). New York: Basic Books.

Thomas, P. L. (2016, August 3). Failing still to address poverty directly: growth mindset as deficit ideology [Web post]. Retrieved from https://radicalscholarship.wordpress.com/2016/08/08/failing-still-to-address-poverty-directly-growth-mindset-as-deficit-ideology/.

Tozer, S., Senese, G., & Violas, P. (2013). *School and society: Historical and contemporary perspectives,* 7th ed. New York: McGraw-Hill.

Utt, J. (2012). How To Talk About Privilege To Someone Who Doesn't Know What That Is. *Everyday Feminism.* Retrieved April 1, 2018, from https://everydayfeminism.com/2012/12/how-to-talk-to-someone-about-privilege/.

Wallace, D. F. (2009). *This is water: Some thoughts, delivered on a significant occasion, about living a compassionate life.* New York: Little, Brown and Company.

Yoon, I. H. (2006). Trading stories: Middle-class white women teachers and the creation of collective narratives about students and families in a diverse elementary school. *Teachers College Record, 18*(2): 1–54.

Young, I. M. (2009). Five faces of oppression. In M. Adams, W. J. Blumenfeld, H. W. Hackman, M. L. Peters, & X. Zuniga (Eds.), *Readings for diversity and social justice, 3rd ed.* (pp. 3–22). New York: Routledge. https://doi.org/10.1017/CBO9781107415324.004.

Contributors

(in order of appearance)

Andrea M. Hyde, Ph.D. (Quad Cities, IA/IL), is a professor in the Department of Educational Studies at Western Illinois University where she teaches courses in the social foundations of education, education policy, and qualitative research. Andrea studies school-based yoga curriculum and teacher training programs, and relates this work to critical pedagogy and social justice education. She has also developed a mindfulness pedagogy for post-secondary education, with connections to philosophy of education and critical social theories. As a consultant and program evaluator for Yoga in Schools, Andrea helped to design and evaluate grant-supported, standard-aligned, professional development programs for teachers in the use of yoga techniques as part of their Physical Education and Health classes. Andrea is also certified to teach yoga to both children and adults.

Janet D. Johnson, Ph.D., RYT-200 (Providence, RI), is a professor of secondary education and Site Director of the Rhode Island Writing Project at Rhode Island College. She teaches undergraduate courses in English education and gender and women's studies, and teaches graduate courses in teacher research and qualitative inquiry. With extensive experience working in schools as a researcher and supervisor of teacher candidates, she has done a number of qualitative studies on social justice and critical literacy. She recently conducted a year-long qualitative study of a yoga class in an urban high school. Janet is a certified yoga teacher and teaches on a weekly basis.

Helene McGlauflin, M.Ed., LCPC, KYT (Brunswick, ME), is a counselor, yoga teacher, and writer. She has an M.Ed. in counselor education, is a licensed clinical counselor, a certified yoga teacher, and a writer of poetry, fiction, and nonfiction. Helene has been an educator for 35 years and has brought mindfulness and yoga practices to a public elementary school in midcoast Maine where she is a counselor through her class *Calm and Alert*. Her book *Calm and Alert: Yoga and Mindfulness Practices to Teach Self-regulation and Social Skills to Children* was published in 2018.

Debra A. Krodman-Collins, Ph.D. (Broward County, FL), is a licensed psychologist, a licensed and nationally certified school psychologist, and a registered yoga teacher. Debra's collaboration on the S.T.O.P. and Relax program was inspired by her work with children with autism spectrum disorders in Broward County Public Schools where she works.

Lindsay Meeker, Ed.D. (Quad Cities, IA/IL), is the Director of English Learners in the Wheaton School District. She is a former English as a Second Language teacher and Literacy Coach. Lindsay has trained teachers in the Kagan Cooperative Learning system, CRISS Strategies, ESL strategies, and was named a Master Teacher by the Moline Dispatch in 2016. Lindsay teaches professional development workshops for teachers in Yoga and Mindfulness in the classroom and wrote her dissertation on studying kindergarteners' responses to school yoga.

Lisa Flynn, E-RYT 500 (Dover, NH), is the founder and director of ChildLight Yoga and Yoga4Classrooms, organizations providing evidence-informed yoga and mindfulness education to children, as well as training and support for thousands of educators, kids yoga teachers, and professionals worldwide. She serves as a curriculum consultant and speaks regularly at yoga, mindfulness, education, and school counseling conferences, as well as schools and yoga centers around the country. She is also a respected leader and collaborator in the school yoga and mindfulness movement and greater kids yoga community internationally.

Carla Tantillo Philibert, M.S.Ed. (Chicago, IL), founder of Mindful Practices, is also an international presenter, consultant, teacher, yogi, devoted mother and wife, and dog lover. She conducts professional development trainings nationally. Carla is the author of *Cooling Down Your Classroom,*

Student Wellness in 8–10 Minutes Each Day, as well as three books on Everyday SEL for Elementary, Middle and High School.

Peggy C. Collings, M.S.Ed. (Chicago, IL), taught middle grades in Chicago and its suburbs for twelve years. She holds a Bachelor's degree from Northwestern University's Medill School of Journalism and a Master of Education degree from DePaul University in Chicago. She has been part of the Mindful Practices team since 2015.

Dee Marie, M.A., CYT (Boulder, CO) was a professional dancer in New York City when she was hit by a taxi and told she would never walk again at age 26. She later received her Master's degree in Child and Motor Development from NYU and was certified as an adult yoga teacher, prenatal and children's yoga teacher. She is a practicing yoga therapist trained by Swami Rama and Mukunda Stiles since 1986. She created CALMING KIDS, a 501(c)(3) non-profit organization, in 2004, to address bullying.

Michelle Brook, RYT-200 (Jersey City, NJ) has a 200-hour RYT certification from the American Yoga Academy and a 30-hour certification from Karma Kids Yoga Studio in NYC. She continues her education with online certificate courses in Neuroscience, Physiology, Biology, Nutrition, and Niroga Institute's Transformative Life Skills Training. She teaches kids yoga classes at the New York Sports Club in Butler, NJ, Bloom Yoga in Fairlawn, NJ, and in private homes. For many years Michelle has been teaching preschool nature programs, grade school river ecology lessons, and doing substitute teaching at all grade levels. Recently she initiated a yoga program in a Jersey City elementary school.

Joanne Spence, BSW, ERYT, LFYP-2 (Pittsburgh, PA) is a social worker, yoga teacher, and an international speaker/trainer for health and wellness. She is the director of Urban Oasis Pittsburgh, a yoga therapy studio in Pittsburgh's East End, and the Founder and Executive Director of Yoga in Schools, a nonprofit organization that currently reaches over 20,000 children with innovative children's yoga programming as part of Physical Education to schools both locally and nationally.

Peg Oliveira, Ph.D., E-RYT 500 (New Haven, CT) is deputy director of the Gesell Institute of Child Development and consults for Connecticut's

Office of Early Childhood. She is the founder and executive director of 108 Monkeys, a nonprofit yoga service organization based in New Haven, Connecticut. She believes in yoga as the great equalizer and that practicing yoga means practicing justice.

Index